The Playbook:
Dispatches from a Life Still Under Construction

Daniel C. Haynes

DEDICATION

To those who crossed the wilderness without a map, and to the players who spent entire seasons on the sideline waiting for a whistle that never came.

To the builders with dirt beneath their nails and hope lodged deep in their chests, who stopped waiting for permission and began constructing lives strong enough to carry the weight of their calling.

And to Debbie, who built the court before I knew how to play, who taught me that talent may strike the spark, but character is what sustains the fire, and who loved me faithfully while I was still under construction.

This Playbook is for those still becoming in every season, at every stage, with hands in the work and eyes fixed forward.

CONTENTS

FOREWORD

It has been my privilege to serve as Daniel Haynes's pastor at Church City USA. Over the years, I have watched his character mature, his faith deepen, and his desire sharpen to use what God has placed in him for the benefit of others. One quality that has consistently stood out is his love for writing.

For Daniel, writing is not a casual interest; it is a calling. He not only wants to communicate clearly, but to help others grow in their ability to express themselves with honesty and strength.

That heart is evident throughout this book. Daniel shares pieces of his story—his struggles, his growth, and the faith in Jesus Christ that has sustained him and shaped the way he sees life. His transparency invites the reader to connect not only with the lessons, but with the journey behind them. He writes to offer encouragement, insight, and healing to those who read.

Readers will also find practical wisdom that can produce real change when applied consistently. There is a therapeutic element to this work as well. As you read, you may find yourself reflecting on your own patterns, gaining clarity about why you are in certain situations, and identifying what may have contributed to them. That kind of honest reflection can be challenging, but it is also deeply rewarding.

A strength of this book is Daniel's use of Scripture. Each chapter begins with a biblical passage that anchors the lesson being presented. While he may not explore every theological detail of each text, he faithfully draws out the practical wisdom Scripture offers and demonstrates how it can be lived out day by day. Just as importantly, he leaves readers with an invitation to return to those passages and discover their richness more fully.

Another thoughtful feature is the space Daniel provides for personal reflection. After each chapter, readers are given an opportunity to write, process, and take honest stock of their own lives. This turns the book from something you simply read into something you actively engage.

Because of that, it can function as a devotional, an encouraging read, a personal workbook, or a window into Daniel's journey. The structure carries the reader from practical instruction into deeper spiritual examination.

What I appreciate most about Daniel's message is the balance he maintains between pursuing purpose and honoring proper priorities. This book reminds us that ambition and calling matter, but they must never come at the expense of our relationship with Jesus Christ. When our walk with Him is in order, everything else begins to fall into its proper place. Without Him, even our greatest achievements can leave us empty.

My prayer is that this book will encourage you, strengthen your faith, and lead you into a deeper walk with our Lord Jesus Christ.

Pastor Richard Ishmael
Church City USA

A Note on This Book

Most books choose between telling you a story and giving you something to do with it. This one refuses to choose.

What you are holding is a formation memoir and a playbook—both at once, neither one subordinate to the other. The memoir half is specific: one life, one set of seasons, two continents, thirty years. The names are real. The costs were real. The failures are in here with their full weight, not softened into lessons after the fact. I am not writing from the summit of a life that has been resolved. I am writing from the middle of one that is still being built.

The playbook half is what the memoir earns. Not what I extracted from it after the fact and arranged into a framework—what the seasons themselves produced. Each chapter is a field report. Each Running the Play section is a set of plays drawn from that report and handed to you to run in yours. You can read straight through and return to the exercises later, or work through each one as you go. But a playbook that stays on the shelf is just paper. At some point it has to get dirty.

One practical note. These chapters do not all start from the same place, and neither do readers. If you are carrying a mistake you cannot put down, go to Chapter 16. If you are waiting on a door that has not opened, go to Chapter 22. If you are depleted and not sure how you got there, go to Chapter 17. If you have been carrying everything alone, go to Chapter 13. If you know what you are supposed to do and cannot make yourself move, go to Chapter 11. And if you don't know where you are—start at Chapter 1 and let the book find you.

Whatever brought you here is already part of the formation.

Let's run the play.

PROLOGUE

The Boy at the Airport

To the five-year-old boy standing at the airport:

Dear Daniel,

I'm writing to you as you stand at the airport at the age of five, trying to understand what's happening around you. You're watching someone else leave, someone you love, someone who promised not to leave, and you're wondering—"Why do people always leave? What's wrong with me?"

I see you fighting to rationalize what's next, even though you're just a child. You don't realize it yet, but that curious mind of yours is already moving so many steps ahead, leaping to places it doesn't need to go. You're trying to piece together a world that feels broken, but in doing so, you're stuffing emotions and feelings down so deep that if anyone were to dig, it would cause you to crumble.

Twenty-three years later, I'm writing to you from a place far removed from that Ogle home where you caught grasshoppers and looked out at the endless skies. I wish I could hold your hand and tell you this face-to-face, but here's what I can say: you'll make it to the place you told Aunty Debbie you'd be. You'll live in that city you dreamed about, earning scholarships you didn't think were possible.

But boy, Daniel, it won't be easy. Not one bit. You're a fighter—and that's a beautiful thing—but sometimes the weight of your decisions will hang heavy on your shoulders, almost too heavy to bear. Even now, as I write this, I feel it. You feel it too, don't you? How everything seems so serious, so drastic when you make a decision? I know you do.

There's so much I want to say to you—lessons I wish I could teach you now, warnings I wish I could give. But more than anything, I want you to know you'll be okay. You'll be more than okay. You'll endure, you'll thrive, and you'll find a strength you didn't know you had.

But listen closely, Daniel. Here are some things I need you to know. These lessons will keep you safe. They'll keep you grounded. And they'll guide you closer to the Almighty—the one who has been pulling at your heart all along.

Stay close to God. *I'm not being cliché, and I'm not trying to scare you. I know there are mornings when you wake up terrified, wondering if the rapture happened and you were left behind. But Daniel, you'll never have to live with that fear as long as you stay close to Him. He's not distant. He's right there, holding you—even when you don't feel it. Trust Him. He'll be your anchor when the storms of life rage.*

Guard your heart. *I know you. I am you. You love so deeply, so fully, that it consumes you. You give and give, hoping for the same love in return, and when you don't feel it—when you think you're not getting it—you lash out. Or worse, you pull away and retreat into yourself. Stop. You don't have to. Breathe, Daniel. Do things because you want to, not because you're trying to earn someone's love, approval, or praise. You're not on stage. Leave the applause for the theater. God's approval is the only one that matters.*

Always tell the truth and act with integrity. *Lies have a way of eating at you from the inside. You've already seen it, haven't you? The whispered secrets, the exchanged glances, the things left unsaid when you ask the "wrong" questions. Don't let that be your story. Live with integrity, Daniel. Speak truth, even when it's hard. Especially when it's hard. Truth will be your shield, and integrity will be your strength.*

Listen to Debbie. *I know. I know. She's not your mother, and you don't want to call her "Mommy." But one day, you will. And when you do, you'll realize she's been right about so many things. Her words—no matter how firm or frustrating they feel now—are rooted in love. She's preparing you for what's ahead, even when you don't understand. Trust her wisdom. It will guide you.*

Trust your instinct. *That little voice inside you, the one that screams "danger"—listen to it. Don't let the fleeting pleasures of the night dull that voice. Don't silence your conscience. Your spirit knows right from wrong, Daniel. Trust it. And when you fail—and you will—I want you to know this: I forgive you. I've already laid it all at the foot of the cross. God has forgiven us, and so I forgive us too.*

Truth be told, Daniel, there's so much I wish I could say. So many things I want to warn you about, so many things I want to help you avoid. But then again, maybe this version of us wouldn't exist if I did.

Your dreams, Daniel, are precious. They'll carry you through the darkest nights. They'll give you something to hold onto when everything else feels impossible. But don't forget to give those dreams to God. Let Him guide them. Let Him take them further than you ever could on your own. He'll protect you. He'll be your shield and your strength. Let Him use you. Make Him proud.

I love you, Daniel and I'm proud of you.
Even now.
Be proud of yourself too.

With love and hope,
Daniel (23 years later)

But before the letter, there was the bench. He does not remember the airport the way adults remember things. He was five. What he remembers is feeling. The schoolyard empty in a way schoolyards are not supposed to be empty. The bench at the gate where he had sat long enough for the waiting to feel permanent.

Guyana's afternoon light made empty spaces look final. The shadows lengthened, and the sounds of the school day—voices, bells, the scatter of feet—gave way to the kind of quiet five-year-olds are not equipped to interpret. He only knew that everyone else had gone, and he had not, and that each sound from the road—an engine, a gate, footsteps—arrived with a small surge of hope that reset itself when it turned out to be nothing.

Every sound from the road was Debbie arriving. Every sound from the road was not Debbie arriving. She came. She had run late. She came, and the waiting ended.

What he remembers is the waiting. The bench. The lengthening shadows.
The small surge and reset of hope until it was no longer necessary.
And somewhere in that waiting, a five-year-old boy made a quiet decision he would not recognize as a decision: that he was fine. That he could carry this.

It was the first lie, and it fit so perfectly he forgot it was a lie almost immediately. This book is the work of undoing what he decided on that bench.

~ ~ ~

That letter sat with me for a long time after I wrote it in 2024. I read it back and felt something I hadn't expected: not nostalgia, but clarity. The five-year-old who asked why people leave had been answered. Not all at once, and not easily—but answered. And in between that airport and this page, the chapters of this book had slowly, painfully, accumulated. Not in a notebook. Not in a seminar. In seasons.

That letter was the beginning. It was the first time I tried to speak to the parts of myself that were still trapped in the airport, still wondering why people leave, still trying to earn love through performance. I wrote that letter to the boy who was surviving. I wrote this book for the man who is building.

Survival taught me grit. It taught me resilience. But survival has a ceiling. Survival can keep you alive, but it cannot build you a legacy.

There came a point in my life—somewhere between the late nights of grad school, the heartbreak of closed doors, and the quiet pressure of turning thirty—when I realized that pushing through was no longer enough. I didn't need more motivation; I had plenty of fire. I didn't need more opportunity; doors were opening. I needed a playbook.

These chapters are that record—field notes from what it has actually taken to move from surviving to building. They are not complete. They are not finished. They are the inheritance of a life still under construction.

—Daniel C. Haynes

PART I
ORIGINS

Identity, honesty, endurance:
Who must you become before the game begins?

CHAPTER ONE

Eight Christmases

"Let us run with endurance the race that is set before us."
—Hebrews 12:1

For eight Christmases, I told myself the same story. On this one, I sat alone in my apartment with my cat, Suki, quietly taking inventory of the years behind me—the emotions, the locations, the widening distance between who I had been and who I believed I was becoming.

I could have chronicled each Christmas in detail since leaving Guyana's shores for the city that never sleeps—how rainforest greens gave way to concrete and steel, how familiarity became ambition, and ambition hardened into endurance. But as the lights on my first Christmas tree blinked softly in yellow, I realized something else. I had been telling my story quietly, almost reverently, as though repetition might eventually turn it into truth.

It was a story of resilience and survival. Of perseverance and grit. A story anchored to one central belief: that this was temporary, that my circumstances would shift, that next year would be different, that endurance would be enough. Each December arrived dressed in promise. Each January left me with the same unspoken questions: *"Why was I still here? What was I actually hoping to accomplish? Who was I becoming? Was this really my life?"*

I wasn't failing in obvious ways. I was working, showing up, doing what responsible people do when they don't yet know what else to do. I was doing what Granddad from The Boondocks says when Huey asks him, *"What do you do when you can't do nothing, but there's nothing you can do?"*

His answer, *"You do what you can."*

And I was. From the outside, my life looked stable—commendable, even. The degrees, the books, the rooms I entered and held, the network I had built. But from the inside, something was eroding. I had learned how to survive seasons. I had not learned how to complete them.

I ran false laps for years.

When I finally sat with my own life, they became impossible to ignore. I told myself I was being faithful—and I was, but faithful to performance. Faithful to appearing strong. Faithful to showing up as the "best version" of myself before I even knew what that meant. I called cowardice bravery. What I was really being was afraid—afraid of what finishing would force me to admit: that I had outgrown certain races, misjudged distances, and let endurance without direction quietly harden into inertia.

Detours only become wisdom when they are named. Otherwise, they repeat. As I write this, I can still hear Debbie's voice saying what she always did: *"If you don't learn the lesson, you're doomed to repeat the class."*

There is a particular kind of shame that comes not from failing, but from recognizing how long you've been failing to see. I didn't leave races dramatically. I drifted from them. I kept the language of commitment while quietly withdrawing the energy. I was present in all the visible ways and absent in the only way that mattered.

When I finally came back—not to every race I'd walked away from, but to the ones that still had my name on them—the hardest part wasn't starting again. It was resisting the urge to announce it. To make the return a performance, another story of resilience. I had to learn to come back quietly. No speeches. No reinvention. Just a return to the lane.

I'm still learning what finishing means. Some seasons, it looks like endurance. Others, it looks like release—setting down what was never mine to carry in the first place. What I know now is that the two are not the same. And knowing that difference cost me eight Christmases to learn.

What This Season Left Me

Survival is a gift until it becomes a ceiling. I spent years grateful to be enduring, not real-izing that endurance without direction had become its own kind of avoidance. The race was never the problem. My refusal to tell the truth about which race I was actually run-ning was.

Windowsill Reflections

• What race did you begin with pure intent—and when did it quietly be-come about proving something?
• Is this season forming you—or erasing you?
• Where are you in survival mode right now, and what is it preventing you from seeing?
• What would re-entry look like if you refused self-condemnation and chose humility instead?
• If you finished this race, what part of your identity would finally become trustworthy to you?

Benediction

Finish what was entrusted to you—quietly, faithfully, and without leaving your lane.

Running the Play

Identify One Abandoned Race. Complete this sentence with precision:

"I started _______________________________________ but

I left the race when _______________________________."

Define "Finishing" in This Season. What does finishing look like now, with your current capacity? What is the smallest faithful version of comple-tion?

____

____

Name Your Default Exit. Choose one: distraction, shame, bitterness, survival mode, reinvention.

My default exit is:

____

The Seven-Day Return Plan. Choose one concrete action you will take within the next seven days.

Date: ________________________   Time: ________________________

Action:

____

____

____

Accountability (who will know?): __________________________________

One Line of Worship. Write one sentence you can pray without performance:

"God, I will finish ____

as an act of ____."

CHAPTER TWO

The Word I Refused

"Search me, O God, and know my heart; try me and know my thoughts; and see if there be any grievous way in me and lead me in the way everlasting."—Psalm 139:23–24

The word was not hurled at me. It was not shouted, sharpened, or weaponized. It was said plainly—almost gently—in a conversation that had no intention of undoing me. And that, more than anything, is why it stopped me.

I felt my reaction before I understood it. A tightening. A quiet defensiveness rising in my chest. The kind that arrives before reason has time to intervene.

The word was **victim**.

I did not hear it as description. I heard it as accusation. To me, it sounded like weakness, passivity, surrender. It felt incompatible with the story I had told myself about who I was: resilient, disciplined, self-made. Someone who endured. Someone who survived.

As a child, I grew up hearing, "Sticks and stones may break my bones, but words will never hurt me." It lived on playgrounds and in classrooms, anywhere language was thrown like something meant to bruise. I heard it on television too, and before long I was saying it myself, as if repetition could make it true.

I have never broken a bone. I have sprained and fractured them, torn ligaments, carried the sharp, clean ache of physical pain. But physical pain has always felt honest to me—direct, measurable, finite. Words are different. Words can bruise invisibly, linger quietly, and return years later with the same force, as though time never passed.

Some words move across us without resistance. Some embolden. Some lift. And then there are words that stop us cold—not because they are false, but because they are close enough to the truth to threaten whatever we have been using to stay standing.

For me, **victim** was one of those words.

As an immigrant, you learn quickly how to braid survival into identity, carrying optimism and fear in the same suitcase. So, when the word appeared—spoken casually, almost clinically—I rejected it immediately.

That's not me.

At the time, I thought I was defending myself, pushing back against a description that made me feel smaller than I was. Looking back, I can see it more clearly: I was not only rejecting a word. I was protecting a version of myself I had already outgrown, not yet knowing how to grieve the change.

I built more than a few blind spots over the course of my life, and some of them looked virtuous from the outside. Some of them even sounded like wisdom. That is what makes them so difficult to surrender. We defend them. We justify them. We spiritualize them. Then we wonder why growth stalls, why we keep returning to the same wall, why the same patterns keep changing clothes but never leave the room.

My breakthrough did not come through confrontation. It came through definition.

When I was a boy and encountered a new word—or even a familiar word I could not fully define—Debbie would tell me to grab a dictionary and look it up. It was a practice I carried into adulthood, and later into my own life as a teacher: define first, then speak.

So when I finally sat down with the word *victim,* I did the same thing. Not to agree with it. Not to internalize it. Simply to define it, and to stop negotiating with myself in vagueness.

Victim: one who is harmed, injured, or killed as a result of a crime, accident, or other event or action.

No accusation. No moral judgment. Just fact.

And there it was—the truth I had been avoiding. I had been harmed.

That fact explained something about my history, not my destiny. I was not helpless. I was not powerless. But I had been harmed. And like many people who have learned to survive, I had trained myself to minimize what hurt me because naming it felt too close to surrender.

I was not lying. But I was not telling the whole truth either.

Some people build their entire identities around victimhood. It becomes the lens through which everything is interpreted. But my problem was different. I built my identity around being the opposite—the one who does not break, does not need, does not stop.

I did not need the word *victim* to define me completely. I needed to admit it described me partly—if only ten percent of me.

That small admission was enough to loosen my grip on a story that had once protected me but was now limiting me. It made room for complexity. It made room for honesty. It made room for a self that did not have to be invincible in order to be worthy.

The most dangerous lies are not the ones that are entirely false. They are the ones that are mostly true—true enough to keep you loyal, incomplete enough to keep you stuck.

Strength is a gift. A hard-won gift. But I had let it harden into armor. Resilience had become distance, keeping out the very people capable of seeing and knowing me. Discipline had become avoidance, my schedule filled so completely that there was no room for truth to surface. And faith, perhaps most dangerously, had become a way to bypass the work of naming pain altogether.

"I'm fine. God has me. Others have it worse." Sometimes that is faith. Repeated often enough, it becomes fear wearing spiritual language.

I still carry some of those tendencies. What changed is that I can name them now. And naming them, even reluctantly, is what finally made room for something to shift.

What This Season Left Me

The word I feared most turned out to be the word I most needed. Not because it named everything, but because it named enough. Ten percent was enough to loosen a story I had been protecting at the cost of my own healing. I have learned since that breakthroughs rarely come through confrontation. More often, they come through precision—the willingness to stop negotiating with vagueness and let a thing be exactly what it is.

Windowsill Reflections

- Which word triggers you most—and why?
- What identity are you protecting when you reject it?
- How has strength doubled as avoidance in your life?
- What truth might God be inviting you into through discomfort?
- Who would you become if you allowed a more honest story?

Benediction

May you have the courage to define what you have been refusing to name. May you find the word you feared is smaller than the freedom waiting on the other side of saying it. The truth does not break you. It simply asks you to put down what was already too heavy to carry.

Running the Play

Identify a Trigger Word. Write down one word that makes you defensive when applied to you. (Examples: victim, controlling, needy, arrogant, avoidant).

_____________________________________.

Define Before You Defend. Look the word up. Write the definition exactly as it appears—without commentary.

Find the Ten Percent. Write one memory, behavior, or pattern where this word is partly true. Not all. Just some.

____

____

____

Name the Cost of Avoidance. What has refusing this word protected you from? What has it cost you?

____

____

____

Choose a New Response. Complete this sentence:

"If this is partly true, then I can __________________________________."

CHAPTER THREE

Carry Each Other

"Carry each other's burdens, and in this way, you will fulfill the law of Christ."—Galatians 6:2

I did not learn who I was, or become anything I am, by myself or by my own strength. I had always known that in theory. The depth of it came slowly, however, and only after I spent years telling a different story—one where endurance was framed as independence, survival was mistaken for strength, and asking for help felt like failure dressed up as humility.

Growing up, I spent much of my time in the pleasure of my own company. Even so, I was never alone. I was surrounded by people: chosen family, neighbors whose homes I spent hours in, church members who encouraged my spiritual growth, teachers who saw potential before I could name it, teammates who went into battle with me—on the cricket field and on the hardwood.

Voices called my name across rooms, across streets, across seasons. In Guyana, no one truly belongs only to themselves. Life spills outward there. What you eat, where you sit, how you grow—none of it happens in isolation. You are watched. You are corrected. You are carried.

Community is engraved into you there. I still remember the way adults spoke with a kind of public guardianship—how someone could catch you doing something you had no right to do and call out, sharp and familiar: *"Boy, your mother know you out here acting like this?"* You were never anonymous. Not really. You belonged to people.

Then I moved.

New York teaches you something different: how to make yourself small enough to fit into crowded spaces without ever touching anyone. How to move efficiently without being known. How to be surrounded and still alone.

A few months into my life here, I watched an elderly man collapse on the street. My Guyanese instinct screamed, call for help—and I did—but what stayed with me was what happened around me. People moved around him and kept going, as if the city had trained them to protect their pace at all costs, even from compassion.

I learned quickly that self-sufficiency is rewarded here. Independence became a badge. It became a language. I wore and spoke both fluently.

At first, it felt like progress. I was doing it. I was making it. I was holding my own. I learned how to carry weight without complaint, how to keep showing up even when no one noticed, how to take pride in quiet sentences: *"I've got this. It's just me here."*

What I did not realize at the time was that I was taking pride in an identity built on isolation.

On the anniversary of my first year in New York, I got a tattoo on my shoulder—a wolf formed by a tree. It signified, and in some ways solidified, that identity: the lone wolf, still tethered to his Guyanese roots

But over time, something else crept in—subtler than exhaustion, quieter even than resentment. I began to feel the cost of carrying everything alone. Not as a dramatic collapse, but as small absences: conversations that stayed on the surface and never ventured deep, joy that felt incomplete, success that arrived without anyone to truly share it with.

Sometimes I would go to the top of the parking garage at St. John's University and stand there, staring into the distance at the Manhattan skyline. Sometimes tears streamed down my face. Sometimes I shouted silently inside my chest, afraid of being heard and more afraid of not being heard at all. Sometimes I wanted one person to hold me—hug me—tell me it would be alright.

I told myself this was the price of adulthood. Of ambition. Of becoming someone. But beneath that explanation lived another truth I was slow to name: **I was growing efficient at surviving and inefficient at belonging.**

There was a season—my second year in New York, the hardest one—when that pattern finally broke. Not dramatically. It happened in a phone call I almost did not make.

I had been carrying something for weeks that I had not named to anyone. A decision I could not make alone. A weight that was starting to bend me sideways. I sat with my phone in my hand for a long time before I dialed. The person I called was not someone I spoke to every day. But they were someone who had known me before New York, before the lone-wolf tattoo, before I learned to perform composure.

I do not remember the exact words I said. I remember that I stumbled through them. I remember that I cried, which I had not done in front of another person in longer than I could account for. And I remember what they said after I finished:

"Why did you wait so long?"

I did not have a good answer. The honest answer was that I had confused needing people with failing them—as if admitting I could not carry something alone was a betrayal of everyone who had believed I could.

That phone call did not solve the problem I was calling about. But it did something else. It reminded me that I was still someone who could be known. That the distance I had built in New York had not yet become permanent.

And once that distance cracked, I began to notice the moments when something in me loosened—team victories with my resident assistant staff, family gatherings with friends who were becoming family, rooms where laughter rose without effort. In those rooms, I remembered how to breathe differently. How to let go of the weight pressed against my chest.

Those moments never came from achievement. They came from shared labor, from someone else carrying what I could not. They came from offering what I had without calculating the return.

It was in those moments that a South African word I first heard in the 2009 film *Invictus* began to surface again—a word that had always been present, but that I did not need to translate until I left home:

Ubuntu: I am because we are.

At first, I treated it like sentiment. Like a cultural artifact. Something poetic but impractical in an environment that rewarded individual performance. But the longer I lived on my own, the clearer it became: Ubuntu is not soft. It is demanding.

It asks something of you. It requires sacrifice—real sacrifice—not as loss, but as exchange. You give so that another can stand. You carry so that another can rest. You receive so that you can keep going.

And somewhere in that exchange, something miraculous happens. The self you were protecting begins to soften. The self you were building begins to deepen. You realize that wholeness was never meant to be achieved alone. It cannot be achieved alone.

I did not learn who I was alone. I learned through hands that steadied me. Through voices that corrected me when I was not ready to hear it. Through communities that absorbed my failures and multiplied my growth. Through sacrifices, given and received, that taught me a truth I could not have arrived at by myself:

Strength that does not circulate stagnates, and life that is not shared narrows.

What This Season Left Me

The myth of the self-made life may produce admiration, but it rarely produces joy. I know because I performed it for years—the lone wolf on the parking garage roof, staring at a skyline that had no idea I existed. What finally broke that performance was not a revelation, but a phone call I almost did not make. Community does not simply arrive. You have to choose it, usually at the exact moment when choosing it feels most like losing.

Windowsill Reflections

- Who helped shape you that you rarely acknowledge?
- Where has independence protected you—and where has it isolated you?
- What does sacrifice mean to you now, and how has that definition changed?

- Where might God be inviting you into deeper mutuality?
- What would it look like to let yourself be carried?

Benediction

You are not meant to stand alone. Carry—and allow yourself to be carried.

Running the Play

Map Your Ubuntu Tree. Write down the names of people who carried you at pivotal moments—emotionally, spiritually, practically. Do not rush this.

____

____

____

Name One Sacrifice You've Avoided. What is one thing you've been unwilling to give—time, honesty, help, vulnerability—because you feared the cost?

____

____

Choose One Shared Action. Identify one concrete way you can participate in shared life this week: ask for help, offer help, show up consistently, stay when it would be easier to leave.

____

____

29

____

Release the Transaction. Write this sentence and sit with it:

"I will give _______________________________ without calculating what I receive."

CHAPTER FOUR

Pressuh Does Buss Pipe

"From everyone who has been given much, much will be demanded."
—Luke 12:48

In Guyana, we have a saying: **"Pressuh does buss pipe."** Pressure causes pipes to burst. It is a simple phrase, usually used when someone has been pushed beyond what they can contain. Early in my life, I assumed people were the same—that pressure was a warning sign, not an invitation.

I associated pressure with exhaustion and scrutiny. With the quiet fear that one misstep might expose something unfinished in me—that it would reveal I was unequipped, perhaps all talk. So, when pressure arrived, my instinct was either to endure it silently or outrun it entirely. I believed relief meant absence. That peace could only come once the weight was gone.

Then I became an athlete.

I remember one game in particular. Seconds left on the shot clock, scores tied. The kind of moment where the gym grows louder and narrower at the same time. Everything slows, but nothing feels calm. Legs heavy. Chest tight. Noise everywhere. And yet the real pressure was not the crowd. It was the awareness that whatever happened next would reveal what practice had actually built in me.

In moments like that, no one cares what you meant to do. No one grades your potential. Pressure strips you down to what is present. Your habits. Your preparation. Your composure. Your honesty. It shows you, without flattery, what is actually there.

I learned quickly that pressure is where truth shows up. Not intention. Not potential. Truth. Who you are—and what you know—reveals itself under strain.

Years later, especially during my time away from home, I began to notice a pattern. The seasons of my life that carried the most pressure were also the seasons in which something meaningful was being asked of me. Not demanded thoughtlessly but entrusted deliberately. Pressure did not arrive randomly. It followed responsibility. Responsibility followed growth. And growth followed capacity. What I had mistaken for a burden was often an assignment.

I saw this most clearly in rooms where expectations were high and excuses were few—classrooms I taught, locker rooms I coached, leadership tables I sat at. Moments where people were not watching to admire, but to rely. Pressure arrived not because I was unworthy, but because someone believed I could hold the weight.

That did not mean life was gentle. I have known moments where circumstances were entirely beyond my control, where uncertainty pressed so tightly against my chest I could barely breathe. I have had more of those moments in the last nine years than in all the years before. And yet, through it all, God carried me.

Where I come from, many never reach the threshold where pressure appears. For some, the doors leading to responsibility never open. For others, the cost feels too steep, and the comfort of complacency becomes a kind of counterfeit peace. To feel pressure at all is to be in the arena. To feel it intensely is to be at the free-throw line with the game on the line— to stand at the intersection of opportunity and responsibility.

I learned this slowly. Sometimes reluctantly. As I grew—academically, creatively, spiritually—ambiguity had less room to hide. The fishbowl effect set in. Expectations sharpened. Tolerance for inconsistency narrowed. Effort alone was no longer enough. What was required was clarity, follow-through, and integrity that could hold under strain.

At first, I resisted this reality. I wanted opportunity without weight. Influence without accountability. Visibility without scrutiny. I wanted the rewards of growth without its demands.

That arrangement does not exist. Pressure is the cost of proximity—to purpose, to leadership, to responsibility that extends beyond yourself. It is the price of being needed.

What changed everything for me was this realization: pressure is not the enemy of peace. Avoidance is. When you run from pressure, you do not remove the weight; you displace it. It resurfaces as anxiety, procrastination, resentment, or quiet self-doubt. The load remains, only now it is unstructured and unmanaged.

In my poetry, I often write about having comfort tested against growth's rubric. Growth has a grading scale. Its exams are the uncomfortable moments that ask more of you than you planned to give. You can opt out. You can fail. But when you accept pressure as part of the assignment, something shifts. You stop asking why it is so hard. You start asking what it is asking of you.

Pressure stops feeling like punishment and begins functioning as instruction. It clarifies priorities. It strips excess. It exposes where preparation is thin and where character is strong. It reveals what you truly rely on when comfort is no longer available.

This is why pressure exposes people. Some harden under it. Some collapse beneath it. Others rise—not because they are extraordinary, but because they remain present while carrying weight. I used to wonder which kind I was. Now I think the wondering itself was part of the answer. The fact that the question mattered to me meant I had not stopped caring about the weight. I had not decided to put it down.

The privilege of pressure is this: your presence matters. Your decisions carry weight. Your integrity affects more than just you. You are not under pressure because you are replaceable. You are under pressure because you are relied upon.

What This Season Left Me

The Guyanese proverb had it right all along: pressure does cause pipes to burst. What I did not understand as a child is that bursting is not always failure. Sometimes it is the release of what was never meant to be held indefinitely. The pressure that refines is different from the pressure that deforms. One is tied to something being built. The other is arbitrary, designed to diminish. Learning to tell the difference took most of my twenties.

Windowsill Reflections

• Where has pressure revealed growth you did not recognize in yourself?
• What weight are you carrying that you secretly resent—and what might it be asking of you instead?
• How do you typically respond to pressure: control, withdrawal, perfectionism, or presence?
• What would it look like to treat pressure as stewardship rather than a threat?

Benediction

May you carry what you have been given without shrinking and steward the weight without surrendering your peace. May pressure clarify you without hardening you and deepen your strength without stealing your rest.

Running the Play

Name the Pressure. Where do you feel it most right now—work, family, calling, leadership, or self-expectation?

Identify the Assignment. What responsibility sits beneath that pressure? Who is affected by how you carry it?

Audit Your Avoidance. How have you been trying to escape the pressure rather than steward it?

____

____

____

Choose One Adjustment. What single boundary, habit, or conversation would help you carry this weight more faithfully?

____

____

____

Reframe the Weight. Complete this sentence:

"This pressure may be revealing that

_______________________________________."

CHAPTER FIVE

No One Can Beat Me but Me

"Which of you, wanting to build a tower, does not first sit down and count the cost, to see if he has enough to complete it?"—Luke 14:28

I have always been competitive. I hated losing—not in theory, but in practice. Sports, video games, cards, dominoes, arguments. It did not matter. Somewhere along the way, I adopted a quiet creed: **no one can beat me but me.** If I lost, it was because I let it happen. If I failed, it was because I misplayed something.

Life eventually corrected that illusion.

I can still remember seasons when I was already celebrating a win in my mind before I had honestly measured what it would require of me. I would picture the door opening, the recognition arriving, the relief of having made it through. I was drawn to the image of arrival long before I had built a life sturdy enough to absorb what arrival would cost. In those moments, I was not asking whether I was ready to carry the thing. I was asking only how quickly I could reach it.

At first, the correction came gently. Athletics taught me that effort does not guarantee outcome, and preparation does not always translate into victory. Loss humbled me on the court and on the field.

But outside those arenas, in the larger decisions of my life, I carried a different posture. There were seasons when I wanted the win more than I wanted to understand why I wanted it. I can see myself clearly now: energized, motivated, convinced that desire itself was evidence of readiness.

When desire felt thin, I compensated with effort. I prayed. I planned. I worked. I told myself I was being responsible. And yet, if I am honest, I was far more in love with the outcome than I was attentive to what it would require of me once it arrived.

I wanted the door to open. I did not linger long enough to ask what I would be carrying through it.

At the time, that pause felt unnecessary. Almost offensive. *What will this cost you?* sounded like someone dimming the lights just as the room was warming. It felt pessimistic. Like fear dressed up as wisdom. Like a question asked by people who had already made peace with smallness.

So I ignored it.

I told myself preparation could come later. That momentum would shape me. That once I arrived, I would become the kind of person capable of holding what I had won. What I did not yet understand is this: victory does not wait for you to grow into it. It arrives as you are. And it always comes with a receipt. Most people never ask to see it.

We do this in ordinary life all the time. When asked if we want the receipt, we wave it away. Or we take it, fold it, and throw it out. The moment feels complete without it. The purchase feels justified. The cost feels abstract.

Victory works the same way. We rehearse the photograph. The announcement. The title. The podium. The moment when effort is vindicated and doubt goes quiet. We fall in love with the image long before we understand the invoice attached to it. By the time the cost appears, we are already emotionally invested in the fantasy of the win.

I know this because I lived it. There were seasons when motivation felt like permission. When wanting something badly enough seemed like proof I was ready for it. In those moments, *what will this cost you?* did not sound wise. It sounded discouraging—like someone trying to talk me out of my dreams just as I was brave enough to want them.

But the question was never meant to kill the dream. It was meant to protect the dreamer. And this is where ambition stops being fantasy and becomes stewardship.

The arena is never empty. Even when you are alone in a room, even when the decision belongs only to you, the voices arrive. Some belong to people you know: mentors, friends, family, skeptics. Others belong to strangers whose words lodged themselves into your self-perception and never quite left. They whisper caution. They roar doubt. They ask, again and again: *Are you sure?*

I have been tempted to answer them. To concede ground before the fight ever began. *You're right. I can't do this. Who am I to try?* But that would have been a different kind of loss—not the loss of a dream, but the loss of alignment. To step out of the ring not because I was defeated, but because I had never agreed to the weight of the gloves.

What separates those who last from those who flame out is not talent, hustle, or confidence. It is consent. It is the sober agreement to carry what success will demand after the applause fades.

Every meaningful win is funded by something else: time spent that cannot be reclaimed, energy redirected away from rest, anonymity surrendered to scrutiny, relationships asked to carry weight they were not built for, margin eliminated, sleep cashed in for progress.

This is not pessimism. It is arithmetic. The danger is not wanting too much. The danger is winning something you were never prepared to carry—not because you were incapable, but because you never counted the cost.

When that happens, the victory becomes a burden. The blessing turns into pressure without consent. The dream becomes something you quietly resent. This is how burnout disguises itself as achievement.

A victory you are not prepared to carry will eventually carry you away from who you were becoming.

What This Season Left Me

I still catch myself rehearsing the photograph before I have read the invoice. The creed I adopted as a boy—no one can beat me but me—was never entirely wrong. What it missed was the second half: and so, I am responsible for what winning will ask of me next. Counting the cost is not pessimism. It is the act of taking your own ambition seriously enough to prepare for its arrival.

Windowsill Reflections

- What victory have you romanticized without counting its cost?
- Where has ambition disguised avoidance of deeper formation?
- What would it mean to succeed without losing yourself?
- What pressure are you carrying without having consciously agreed to it?
- What win, if achieved today, would actually harm you?

Benediction

May you pursue only the victories you are willing to carry, count the cost without fear, and build a life strong enough to sustain its own success.

Running the Play

Name the Win Clearly. What victory are you pursuing? Be specific.

____

____

____

Explain the Invoice. What will this require in time, energy, attention, relationships, and margin?

____

____

____

Check for Consent. Have you agreed to this cost, or have you been hoping it would not apply to you?

____

____

____

Decide with Integrity. Will you prepare to carry this win, or will you redirect because the cost violates something essential?

____

____

____

Commit to One Discipline. Name one habit or boundary that prepares you to carry the weight if the victory comes.

____

____

____

CHAPTER SIX

The Decimal Difference

"For though the righteous fall seven times, they rise again."
—Proverbs 24:16

I completed both my bachelor's and master's degrees at St. John's University, but they belonged to entirely different seasons of my life. My bachelor's years, from Spring 2017 to Spring 2020, were marked by urgency. I had left Guyana with something to prove, and success felt like evidence that leaving home had been justified. My goal was simple and uncompromising: graduate with a 4.0 GPA.

I did earn a 4.0 in several semesters, but when I graduated ahead of schedule, I held a 3.80. Objectively, it was an achievement. Subjectively, it felt like failure. I did not allow myself to celebrate finishing early. I did not account for the depression, the homesickness, or the long nights of isolation that marked my senior year, especially as the COVID-19 pandemic closed the world inward. I focused only on the number. Because success was imperfect, it became invisible to me.

When I returned for my master's degree a year later, from Fall 2021 to Spring 2023, I told myself I would do it differently. I did not. I simply changed the scale. Again, I set the target at perfection. Again, I came close—graduating with a 3.98 GPA while teaching full-time. And again, I withheld celebration. I did not factor in the weight of holding a classroom all day and returning home to write papers and grade seniors' work late into the night. I did not honor the endurance it took to sustain excellence across competing responsibilities.

What I finally saw—only in hindsight—was not a pattern of failure, but a pattern of perfectionism. And it was never really about the degrees. I was not chasing excellence for its own sake. I was still trying to disprove every voice that had ever underestimated me. I was keeping score at an invisible table no one else was watching. Success had become transactional. Failure had become diagnostic. Neither was allowed to be human.

Sometimes it is only through failure—or through the refusal to feel success—that your patterns are revealed.

I used to believe success and failure were opposites. One meant I was doing something right. The other meant I had misstepped, misjudged, or misunderstood myself entirely. Success felt like confirmation. Failure felt like exposure.

For a long time, I organized my life around that distinction. I chased what validated me and quietly avoided what threatened to contradict the story I was telling myself—and others—about who I was becoming. The 3.80 and the 3.98 taught me otherwise.

Some of my most celebrated moments left me unchanged. Some of my most painful failures changed everything. They stripped away illusions I did not know I was protecting. They clarified motives I had never examined. They forced me to sit with questions I had been postponing for years.

The danger was never failure itself. The danger was allowing either outcome to decide who I was allowed to become. That realization did not arrive all at once. I learned it slowly. In classrooms and workplaces. In creative seasons that flourished and others that stalled. In relationships that worked until they did not.

There were moments when success made me complacent, when momentum masqueraded as mastery. There were moments when failure made me rigid, when disappointment hardened into self-doubt or quiet withdrawal.

Both responses shut down learning.

I have watched people succeed early and stop listening. Their wins became shields, protecting them from feedback they no longer wanted to hear. I have also watched people fail once and stop trying, as though a single collapse was all the evidence they needed to disqualify themselves from further effort.

In both cases, the problem was not the outcome. It was the interpretation. Success can inflate. Failure can imprison. Both distort when they are allowed to speak louder than the truth.

I had to learn that success does not mean I am finished, and failure does not mean I am unfit. Both are moments of exposure. Both reveal something about preparation, posture, and pattern. Neither is a verdict. Both are information. And only one lesson from either is truly dangerous: **stopping the work.**

What This Season Left Me

The 3.80 and the 3.98 look like achievements from the outside. From the inside, they were two rounds of the same fight—me versus an invisible table, keeping score for an audience that had long since gone home. What those numbers eventually gave me was not the proof I was chasing. They gave me the pattern. And seeing the pattern was worth more than the decimal I was protecting it with.

Windowsill Reflections

- Where has success made you less curious?
- Where has failure made you less courageous?
- What outcome are you allowing to narrate your worth?
- What would change if you treated both as instructors rather than judges?

Benediction

May you rise after every fall, remain humble in every win, and stay teachable long enough to become who you are being shaped to be.

Running the Play

Name the Outcome. Where have you recently experienced success or failure?

____

____

____

Interrogate the Meaning. What story are you telling yourself about that outcome?

____

____

____

Extract the Lesson. What is this moment teaching you about preparation, habit, or posture?

____

____

____

Choose Openness. What is one adjustment you will make instead of defending or withdrawing?

CHAPTER SEVEN

The J Train

"Therefore, my beloved brothers, be steadfast, immovable, always abounding in the work of the Lord, knowing that in the Lord your labor is not in vain."—1 Corinthians 15:58

I will never forget standing on the J train platform at Broadway Junction, the wind cutting sharply, carving new lines into my face where old stress had once settled. The thought came quickly, uninvited: *"Why am I out in this cold?"*

It was followed just as quickly by another—something Debbie used to say, half joking, half prophetic: Mankind was not created to be this cold. I laughed to myself, a small, silent rebellion against the wind, watching the tree leaves whip frenetically along the platform.

Eight years—eight winters, eight springs, eight summers, eight falls since I left home. By then, I should have been used to it. I should have been prepared for the first breath of winter's wind, the one that always steals something from you when you inhale too fast. But like those leaves, I still shook—sometimes under the cold, sometimes under uncertainty, sometimes under the quiet erosion of endurance itself.

Most often, I shook under the weight of building something meant to last—of storing up treasure where moth and dust cannot reach, even when nothing around me looked permanent or promised return. My journals tell the truth of those seasons. My handwriting changes. Lines tilt. Letters tighten. The body always confesses what the mouth refuses to say.

I learned what anchoring actually meant long before New York. Growing up in Guyana, every holiday Debbie and I traveled to Essequibo to escape the city. We took a speedboat from Parika to Supenaam, crossing the wide mouth of the river. On calm days, the crossing was beautiful. On rough days, it was merciless. The bow slammed into waves. Rain stung your face. Sometimes we were lifted from our seats only to crash back down as the river reminded us who was in charge.

There was no controlling it. There was only holding fast.

I have had more moments than I can count when endurance was the only thing keeping me in the water, and conviction was the only thing telling me where I was headed.

Endurance keeps you present. Conviction gives you direction. And it matters deeply to know the difference. You can be immovable and still be lost. You can withstand a storm and still drift miles off course. You can survive and still lose yourself.

Conviction is what refuses to negotiate the core of who you are when conditions deteriorate. It is the inner line you will not cross even when compromise looks like relief.

There will be seasons when holding fast feels indistinguishable from stubbornness, when staying true costs you speed, approval, or comfort. There will be moments when it would be easier to soften the edges of what you believe, to dilute your language, or to blur your boundaries just enough to make the resistance stop.

This is where many people lose themselves—not in collapse, but in quiet accommodation. Conviction rarely announces itself. It does not shout, posture, or perform. It simply remains.

For some, convictions are inherited from family, shaped by culture, or assembled from the loudest voices in the room. For others, they are traded depending on which way the wind is blowing.

For me, conviction comes from faith—not faith as performance or polish, but faith as orientation. A belief that my life is not self-authored. A belief that what I am building answers to Someone greater than me. A belief that the dreams placed in my heart were not accidents, and that their fulfillment is not the ultimate goal. Faithfulness is.

I believe my purpose will one day allow me to hear words that do not come from a crowd, a committee, or a scoreboard: ***"Well done, good and faithful servant."***

Holding fast does not mean clinging to comfort, and staying true does not mean refusing growth. Conviction is not rigidity. It is alignment. It means knowing what you will not sacrifice, even for a win. It means knowing what must remain intact, even if the storm lasts longer than you hoped. It means allowing your life to be shaped but not rewritten.

The wind will come. The river will surge. The platform will feel colder than it should. When it does, endurance will keep your feet planted, and conviction will keep your compass true.

What This Season Left Me

I still have the journals from those eight winters. The handwriting does not lie. You can see the seasons in the slant of the letters, the places where the pen pressed harder than it needed to. What those pages taught me is that endurance and conviction are not the same thing, and mistaking one for the other is how you spend years surviving in a direction you never chose. Endurance gets you through the night. Conviction tells you which morning to wake up for.

Windowsill Reflections

- Where have you mistaken endurance for direction?
- What truth are you being asked to hold when letting go would feel easier?
- Which convictions feel most costly right now—and why?
- What would staying true look like if no one ever applauded it?

Benediction

May you remain steady when the wind rises, anchored when the waters surge, and faithful to what you were entrusted with—long after the storm passes.

Running the Play

Name What You're Holding. Write down the convictions you refuse to release, even under pressure.

____

____

____

Identify the Pressure Point. Where are you most tempted to compromise right now—comfort, approval, speed, security?

____

____

____

Check Alignment. Does your current posture reflect who you believe you are called to be?

____

____

____

Reinforce the Grip. Name one practice, boundary, or rhythm that helps you stay anchored this week.

____

49

____

____

CHAPTER EIGHT

Blending Is Not Becoming

*"The Lord does not look at the things people look at. People look at
the outward appearance, but the Lord looks at the heart."*
—1 Samuel 16:7

For most of my childhood, I was an avid reader. On weekdays, when Debbie picked me up from school, I would be curled up in the front seat reading while she shopped in the markets. Reading steadied me, settled me, and set my imagination free. I admired that the characters I loved could endure, find the truth about themselves through their journeys, and then remain true to themselves.

What I did not know then was that something else was forming quietly inside me—a question lurking beneath the surface: *"What did it mean for you, Daniel, to be true to yourself?"*

That question did not begin in adulthood. It only matured there. I was just a boy trying to understand belonging in a world that felt fluid and unfinished. When I was not reading, afternoons were spent catching grasshoppers in the backyard in Ogle, before I moved and spent them jumping the fence around my grandmother's house in Charlestown, running wild with cousins who understood the quiet resilience of latchkey childhoods. There was no performance then. Only presence.

In my teenage years, talent introduced a different kind of attention. In eighth grade, an entire school chanted my name as I broke records during sports. Over time, leadership followed—captaining teams, representing Georgetown in track and field, cricket, and basketball, and eventually representing Guyana in basketball. I became accustomed to being watched.

But applause teaches you early what parts of yourself are rewarded. Charm worked. Skill worked. Being impressive worked. What no one tells you is that approval always has an appetite.

As I grew older, I found myself navigating spaces that welcomed my gifts, my articulation, my appearance, but not the quieter needs of my soul. Migration sharpened this instinct. Moving alone into a world I had only seen through media taught me how to scan rooms—to read tone, posture, silence. I learned how to be palatable. How to adapt. How to stay safe.

Friends called it versatility. Some called it charisma. A few called it being a chameleon. I called it that myself. And for a while, it worked. I learned how to speak in ways that earned approval. I learned how to disarm with a smile. I learned how to blend like paint on a canvas.

But over time, a truth surfaced that I could no longer ignore: **Blending is not becoming. And survival is not living**.

I began to notice the cost. I lost rooms because I told the truth. I lost friendships because I stood on conviction. I lost relationships because I refused to abandon myself in order to be loved on someone else's terms. I walked away from opportunities that required me to shrink in ways my spirit could not survive—not out of anger or arrogance, but out of the quiet humility that only comes after years of exhausting self-betrayal.

One night, years removed from Guyana, childhood nooks, and the scent of guava-tree leaves floating by my windowsill, I came to this realization in the quiet hours—the kind where sleep refuses to stay, and truth takes advantage of the silence.

It arrived without drama. Without fanfare. Without mercy.

I did not know how much of me I was hiding until life asked me to lead. I sat on the edge of my bed, phone turned off, the room dim. Who am I without the mask? Who am I without the performance? Who am I when there is no audience to reward me for being impressive?

I remember sitting on the Long Island Railroad one evening, traveling to

Penn Station from Jamaica. Headphones in. Notes app open. Heart exhausted in a way sleep could not fix. I realized I was tired—tired of measuring every word as though I were on trial, tired of asking permission to be whole, tired of leaving the best parts of myself at the door.

The train was passing Woodside. I remember watching the station name slide by without really reading it. The notes app was open. I had been trying to write a poem. Nothing came. The car was half-empty, and I was grateful for that, because I had nothing left to perform—not even for strangers.

That was the night I stopped trying to find myself in someone else's approval and started asking a different question: Not "*Who do I need to be for this room?*" But "*What is the one true thing I can do right now that requires no audience?*"

I had been circling those questions for years without naming it. What I had been looking for was not reinvention. It was smaller than that. More demanding than that. A paragraph written without polishing it for someone else's eye. A conversation where I said the hard thing instead of the safe one. A boundary kept when no one was watching.

That was the shape of it. Not a transformation. **A practice**. Not a declaration. **A direction**.

For years, I thought growth would arrive as a dramatic overhaul—a decisive pivot, a bold declaration that restructured everything at once. Real change has never worked that way for me. It has always arrived smaller, quieter, and more exacting. One honest line written in a notebook. One conversation not avoided. One decision made without witnesses or applause.

I have oscillated between two voices my entire life: insecurity and integrity.

Insecurity speaks from the place that hopes someone notices or hopes no one notices the truth of what it carries inside. The voice built on integrity speaks from peace. It accepts flaws, acknowledges deficiencies, and still moves forward. I reached a point where I could no longer tell whether I was speaking because I had something true to say, or because I was afraid of being forgotten.

That is when I learned: **Noise keeps you in rooms you have outgrown. But one true thing sets you free from them**.

The most dangerous person in any room is not the loudest one. It is the person who no longer needs to perform. When I leaned into who I really am, my voice sharpened. The work deepened. The rooms changed. And the people who found me there were looking for the real thing too. Authenticity attracts what imitation never can.

The discipline is not choosing many true things. It is choosing one—and keeping it when motivation disappears. That is how identity stabilizes. That is how integrity stops being an aspiration and becomes a pattern.

What This Season Left Me

The chameleon years were not wasted—they taught me every room I would ever need to read and then showed me why reading rooms is not the same as belonging in them. What the LIRR night gave me was simpler than a revelation: permission to stop circling the question and just answer it. The one true thing was never a destination. It was the next honest move, taken without an audience. It still is.

Windowsill Reflections

- Where have you confused being liked with being aligned?
- What part of yourself have you been leaving at the door?
- Where have you been vague to avoid obedience?
- What one true thing have you been postponing?
- Who benefits when you finally stop performing?

Benediction

May you live unmasked, speak without rehearsal, build without betraying yourself, and find that the one true thing—done quietly, faithfully, without witnesses—is enough to change everything.

Running the Play

Name the Edit. Where are you currently adjusting yourself to fit a space, relationship, or expectation?

Trace the Cost. What has that adjustment protected you from—and what has it quietly taken from you?

Name the One True Thing. What is the smallest honest action you know you need to take right now—without announcing it or managing anyone's response?

Remove the Performance. How can you do this without an audience? Not a declaration. A direction.

Anchor it in Rhythm. When and where will this action live in your week?

Keep it When Motivation Fades. What will help you stay faithful when it stops feeling meaningful?

PART II
THE ARENA

Pressure. Risk. Courage:
How do you move when the stakes are real?

CHAPTER NINE

What Survives the Crossing

"The one who has knowledge uses words with restraint, and whoever has understanding is even-tempered."—Proverbs 17:27

There was a season in my life when I spoke simply to speak. Not because I lacked anything to say, but because I wanted to be someone to everyone. I believed that if I could just find the right words and arrange them carefully enough, I could crack open hearts that had long since sealed shut—especially the ones like mine, closed not from arrogance but from defense.

I thought language could earn me belonging. That eloquence might unlock rooms I was never meant to enter and keep me in places that were never built to hold me. What I had not yet learned was this: **even the truest word will fall flat if it is spoken in the wrong room**.

There is a grief in feeling unseen—I know that one well. But there is another grief, quieter and more corrosive, that comes when you offer your full self to someone who does not have the capacity to receive it. That grief lingers. It creates anxiety in the soul. And eventually, it makes you question your voice entirely.

I remember a conversation—the kind where you have prepared everything you want to say, where you have turned the words over for days, arranged them so carefully they feel airtight. And then you say them.

I watched their face while I spoke—the slight nod, the eyes that stayed patient but had already moved somewhere else, the way the silence after I finished was not the silence of someone thinking but the silence of someone waiting for me to be done.

None of it had landed. Not because I said the wrong thing. Because it was the wrong moment, the wrong room, or the wrong version of myself doing the saying. I walked away from that conversation understanding something I had not before: the problem was never the message. It was my relationship to being heard. I needed the words to land so badly that I had stopped asking whether the soil was ready.

Not every word needs to be said. Not every emotion needs translation. Sometimes feelings are passing, flickering, unfinished. And sometimes what we believe is revelation is still being formed—still ripening inside us.

Wisdom often arrives in the questions we forget to ask ourselves: *"Why am I saying this? What response am I hoping for? Am I offering this because it is true—or because I need to be affirmed?"*

I have had to reckon with moments when I listened only to respond, when I offered my ear just to earn something in return. I have argued not because I was right, but because I was afraid of what it would mean to be wrong. Those patterns did not come from malice. They came from unhealed places—especially the ones that made emotional intimacy feel unsafe.

Healing has taught me that maturity is not having the right answers. It is knowing when not to speak from what is still hurting.

In recent years, I have found myself in different kinds of rooms. In some, I am the mentor—steady, responsible, aware of the weight of my words. In others, I am the mirror—reflecting truths people did not expect to see. And in some rooms, I am the quiet example of what not to do. Each role requires discernment because every room listens differently.

When I think about what it means to truly understand an audience, I return to the example of Jesus. He knew how to read a room. He spoke to crowds in parables and to individuals in whispers. When Mary met Him before Lazarus' tomb and said, "If You had been here, my brother would not have died," He did not defend Himself. He did not explain. He wept

The same man who wept also rebuked the Pharisees, remained silent before Pilate, and chose restraint when spectacle would have been easier. He understood the difference between behavior and burden, between data and desperation. He did not speak to be heard. He spoke from clarity, from alignment, from love. That is the model I follow—and the one that humbles me most.

I have spent years unlearning the instinct to fill silence with sound. Silence once terrified me. I did not know who I was without noise. But in this quieter season of my life, I have learned that impact rarely comes from broadcasting. It comes from discernment. From the sacred pause before you speak. From asking not just What do I want to say? but Who is this truly for?

Words are seeds. And seeds require the right soil. Even the most powerful seed will fail if scattered on hardened ground. I have learned not to plant covenant words in temporary soil. Not to speak destiny into ears that only crave entertainment. Not to scatter what is sacred on ground that cannot sustain it.

There is a difference between a chameleon and a translator. A chameleon changes color to hide. A translator changes language to be understood. Being true to yourself ensures you are speaking the truth. The law of translation ensures the truth actually lands.

You do not water down the message to suit the room—that is people-pleasing.

You tune the frequency so the room can hear the music.

Understanding your audience is not about manipulation. It is about stewardship. About honoring both the word and the listener. About trusting that what you carry is good seed—and refusing to waste it on vanity. This was never about sounding impressive. It was always about being faithful.

What This Season Left Me

The season when I spoke simply to speak cost me rooms I will never get back—relation-ships where I poured the right words into the wrong moment and watched them fall. What I carried out of those losses was simpler than a lesson: the word is not enough on its own. The soil matters. The timing matters. And the version of you doing the speaking matters most of all. Restraint is not silence. It is the discipline of waiting until the word and the moment are ready for each other.

Windowsill Reflections

- Where have you mistaken expression for impact?
- What truth are you offering to people who cannot yet hear it?
- How does silence challenge your sense of worth?
- What might change if you trusted timing as much as truth?

Benediction

May you learn when to speak and when to wait, when to plant and when to rest the seed. May your words find soil worthy of them, and may you trust that faithfulness—not volume—is what makes them grow.

Running the Play

Name the Room. Where are you currently speaking without being received?

Check the Motive. Are you speaking from truth—or from a need to be affirmed?

____

____

____

Practice Restraint. Choose one moment this week to withhold words and observe instead.

____

____

____

Plant Intentionally. Where does your voice actually belong right now?

____

____

____

CHAPTER TEN

Before You Move

"Therefore everyone who hears these words of Mine and puts them into practice is like a wise man who built his house on the rock."
—*Matthew 7:24*

Two years ago, I faced a storm that shook me to my core.

It arrived without warning—or so I thought. Looking back now, I can see that the signs were there. Subtle, but present. Someone close to me even named it plainly months earlier: You need to start preparing. I did not listen.

I was thinking positively but not planning wisely. I had faith, but no structure. And when the dust settled, the only thing I had left was belief. But belief without practice cannot hold weight. Faith without works collapses under pressure.

In full transparency, I lost my job despite being offered a new contract. The story behind that loss is told more fully later in this book—it involved a betrayal I did not see coming and a decision I could not avoid making. What matters here is what the loss revealed: I had been thinking positively but not preparing wisely. I had faith but no structure. And when the dust settled, the only thing I had left was belief. But belief without practice cannot hold weight. Faith without works collapses under pressure. Even so, the storm was not wasted. It ushered in a necessary season of rebuilding. Still, I know now that I could have started from higher ground. I could have spared myself a harsher fall.

There are few feelings more unsettling than knowing something is wrong but being unable to name it. It is not panic. Not fear in its loudest form. It is quieter than that. Subtler. A disturbance you feel more than you think.

An unease that arrives without explanation and refuses to leave.

What makes it worse is when it comes during calm. When your life is finally quiet. When your soul feels steady. When the world appears to be responding to your rhythm. No clouds on the horizon. No crack of thunder. Just a shift in the air. The birds move differently. The silence feels off.

When I have named this feeling out loud in the past, people have often tried to soothe it away. You're overthinking. Or they offer mantras polished for reassurance: Speak life. Manifest the outcome. Visualize the win. And while there is truth in hope and power in vision, I have learned—painfully—that positive thinking is not a substitute for spiritual preparation.

The worst storms I have lived through did not announce themselves. They came quietly. They found my harbor unanchored. They looted my peace, capsized relationships, and left fragments where there had once been structure. I confused optimism with readiness. I traded relationship for repetition. I mistook faith for formula.

What I know now is this: peace does not come from believing everything will turn out fine. Peace comes from knowing that even if it does not, you will not be undone. That kind of peace does not arrive at the last minute. It is cultivated. Watered. Built slowly, in silence, long before it is needed.

Growing up, my primary school teachers repeated a phrase so often it felt like ritual: To fail to prepare is to prepare to fail. I was a bright child with a strong memory, which meant I often coasted. I waited until the last moment. I misjudged how much time and attention things actually required. Back then, I thought preparation was only for exams, speeches, interviews—the obvious moments of evaluation.

Time has taught me otherwise.

Preparation is not merely logistical. It is a spiritual rhythm. It is the quiet, daily act of steadying your soul. Securing your inner life. Making deposits before withdrawals are demanded.

It means healing your inner child before relationships require a maturity you have not yet cultivated. Learning how to let go with grace without losing your grounding. Learning how to lose without losing yourself. Standing firm in convictions long before they are tested publicly.

None of this photographs well. None of it trends. But it builds something that holds. The strongest people I know rarely announce their strength. They do not posture. They do not perform. They show up for themselves first, and then for others—even when escape would be easier. They do not crumble when the winds rise because they have built on rock, not sand.

Preparation does not prevent storms, but it determines whether they dismantle you or reveal your foundation.

So now, even when the skies are clear, I bring an umbrella. Even when everything feels aligned, I ask myself what still needs securing—not out of fear, but out of wisdom. I act early so that hard moments do not find me scrambling but standing.

True strength is not measured by how flawless your plans are. It is measured by how rooted you remain when those plans fall apart.

What This Season Left Me

The job loss was the clearest version of a lesson I had been given before and declined to learn. Someone had told me to prepare. I had chosen faith without structure instead— which is not faith at all, only optimism wearing its clothes. What that season rebuilt in me was not just a career. It was the understanding that you cannot borrow peace from a future that has not arrived yet. You have to build it now, quietly, in the ordinary days when no storm is coming. That is when the foundation either forms or it does not.

Windowsill Reflections

- What signs have you dismissed as overthinking?
- Where have you mistaken optimism for peace?
- What would it look like to prepare without panic?
- How rooted is your life right now—really?

Benediction

May you build quietly while the sun still shines, anchor deeply before the winds arrive, and remain standing—not because the storm spared you, but because you were ready when it came.

Running the Play

Audit Your Foundation. Where in your life are you relying on hope without structure? Identify one area (finances, relationships, spirit) where you are coasting.

____

____

____

Check Your Reserves. What inner resource are you spending without replenishing? Are you draining your patience, your savings, or your solitude?

____

____

____

Name the Delay. What preparation have you delayed because the skies feel clear? Name the task you have been putting off because "everything is fine right now."

____

____

____

Build One Pillar. What small, faithful act of readiness can you begin this week? Make the appointment. Save the dollar. Have the conversation.

____

____

____

CHAPTER ELEVEN

When They Counted Me Out

*"Fight the good fight of the faith. Take hold of the eternal life to which
you were called."—1 Timothy 6:12*

There is a moment that comes when humility stops being quiet and becomes combustible. It is not the moment you realize you are behind. You
usually know that already. The résumé is thinner. The resources are fewer.
The room is colder. The odds are stacked. That part is obvious. The moment comes later—when you realize that being underestimated has ceased
to be a burden and has become an advantage.

For most of my life, I lived in spaces where expectation leaned the wrong
way. Where people assumed limitation before listening for capacity. Early
on, I mistook that posture for something to correct. I tried to be louder.
Clearer. More impressive. I believed the answer was visibility.

I was wrong. **Underdogs do not win by demanding recognition. They
win by choosing timing.**

There is a discipline to being underestimated. A kind of cover that allows
you to train without surveillance, to grow without commentary, to sharpen
without distraction. But that discipline only works if you resist the temptation to apologize for your position.

Fear has never been foreign to me. It has simply changed its costume over
the years. I remember feeling it acutely in an airport on January 23, 2017,
standing in line for immigration before boarding a flight bound for New
York. Fear did not shout then. It felt reasonable, responsible, protective.

I have since learned fear's most reliable strategy: it does not usually arrive
as alarm. It arrives as reasonableness. It does not announce itself as cowardice. It comes dressed in logic, caution, and the quiet voice that says: not

yet, not now, not you.

Years later, on a long drive up the East Coast with Debbie, mile after mile, village after village sliding past the windows, she said something that lodged itself deep enough to follow me for years: *"Talent will take you where only character can keep you."*

She did not stop there.

"Sometimes you only get one chance. One opportunity. And if you don't take it, it may take years to come back around. And sometimes it never does. But not every opportunity should be a yes—especially when the price is your soul."

At the time, I heard it like an athlete. I applied it to training, to games. What I did not yet understand was the difference between clock time and God's time.

The Greeks had two words for time: **Chronos** and **Kairos**. **Chronos** is sequential, ticking, measurable—the calendar on the wall. **Kairos** is the opportune moment, a specific alignment of circumstances that demands action now. Most of us live in Chronos, waiting for a date on the calendar. But God often operates in Kairos. He opens a window. He stirs the water; and when He does, He expects you to step in.

When the opportunity to move to the United States finally came, it took three years of Chronos waiting to materialize. Looking back now, I know why. Had it arrived sooner, I would have wasted it. My talent might have opened doors, but my character would not have been able to sustain what waited on the other side. I needed time—to mature, to deepen my faith, to become someone capable of carrying what I was asking God to give me.

But once that preparation is done, the dynamic shifts. The window opens. And the danger changes from impatience to hesitation.

The year 2025 taught me this lesson with force. It stretched me in every direction—visible growth paired with private doubt, potential translating into purpose, and the weight of turning thirty pressing down.

As I moved through that season, I found myself returning to a phrase we use often in the Caribbean. When someone asks how you are doing, the answer comes half-laughing, half-resigned: *"Ah boy... you know I just pushing. Fighting the good fight of faith."*

But what does that actually mean? Does it mean surviving chaos? Does it mean staying small and pushing until permission arrives? No. That is not faith. That is coping.
Real faith is not a burst of intensity. It is a long obedience. But obedience is not passive. There comes a moment when faith stops looking like endurance and starts looking like movement.

It was March 2025 when I finally gave language to something I had lived by long before I named it. I remember the month not because anything dramatic happened all at once, but because everything felt suspended. Time moved differently. Decisions lingered longer than usual. Even the air seemed to hesitate.

I ended that month with a quiet commitment to continue building legacy—not loudly or defiantly, but faithfully. To keep breathing, writing, and bearing witness. To keep teaching. To keep stepping into spaces that younger versions of myself once only imagined from the outside. That ordinary persistence reminded me of something I had nearly forgotten: **unyielding faith is also a form of courage**.

As Cleo Sol's voice drifted through my apartment and afternoon light turned dust into gold across the windowpane, two questions surfaced and refused to leave:

"Was I being honest about what I was afraid of?"

"Was I failing to recognize the fullness of what stood before me?"

Eventually, you arrive at a moment where you realize the room is stacked against you, the giants are laughing, and the mountain will not move just because you study it.

The underdog mistake is passivity. The underdog myth says: wait your turn, be grateful, stay small until invited. The truth is harsher and holier: there is a moment when waiting becomes disobedience.

In every level of organized sport I have played or coached, the pep talk for the underdog team is always the same: hit them hard, hit them fast, do not give anything, take everything. That principle holds true off the field. You do not wait for an invitation to the table—you flip theirs or build your own. You do not wait for confidence. You move because belief demands action.

We are conditioned to think of risk as recklessness—a cliff, a free fall, a gamble. What they rarely tell us is this: real risk is not a cliff. It is a door. Some never knock. Some knock and walk away when it does not open immediately. Some press their ear to the wood, waiting for a sign. And some turn the handle.

Staying put is not neutral. Inaction is not harmless. Not choosing is still a choice, and avoiding movement is movement in the wrong direction. You can lose years convincing yourself you are being patient when you are actually being afraid.

We live in a culture that romanticizes courage—a Hans Zimmer score, a viral moment, a perfectly timed clapback. But real courage is quieter than that. It is the decision to keep going when the logic says stop.

Real courage looks less like a movie and more like this: a trembling voice that keeps speaking anyway. Clicking post when you know your circle might shun you. Showing up for the job you feel unqualified for. Paying the electric bill with the last money you have. Cleaning your room while a depressive episode presses in.

When clarity meets action and is undergirded by prayer, something shifts. You become dangerous—not to people, but to the forces that thrive on your hesitation.

I have watched people with far more talent hesitate themselves into irrelevance. I have watched fear disguise itself as patience long after the Spirit had already said, "Now." But I have also learned that the most dangerous version of a person is not the one with power. It is the one who has nothing left to lose except their integrity—and refuses to surrender it.

Think of the manna in the wilderness. God provided enough food for the Israelites, but with a strict expiration date. They had to gather it that day. If they tried to hoard it for tomorrow, it rotted. The lesson was clear: God's provision is linked to God's timing. You cannot bank today's anointing for tomorrow's battle.

I have learned that the pain of discipline weighs ounces, but the pain of regret weighs tons. There is no haunting quite like the memory of a shot you did not take because you were too busy aiming.

Do not confuse humility with hesitation. You cannot train forever. At some point, you must step into the game. The foundation has been tested. The window is open. The moment now requires movement.

What This Season Left Me

Eight years separate the airport immigration line from the March 2025 apartment— 2017 and 2025, the same fear in different clothes. What this underdog season taught me is that the pattern does not break on its own. At some point, Chronos runs out and Kairos demands an answer. What I have learned to ask is not whether I am afraid, but whether fear is the one holding the pen. The shot I almost did not take is often the one I am most grateful I took.

Windowsill Reflections

- Where have you mistaken waiting for wisdom when it was actually fear?
- What giant have you been studying instead of confronting?
- Where are you confusing "waiting on God" with "hiding from risk"?
- How does Kairos time change your view of your current season?
- What would it look like to trust God with action, not just belief?

Benediction

May you move when the odds say no, strike when fear says wait, and trust that the God who sent you into the fight has already gone before you. May you recognize the moment when obedience is required, have the courage to move without guarantees, and choose faithfulness while the door is still open.

Running the Play

Name the Odds. Where in your life do the odds feel stacked against you right now? Name it honestly.

____

____

____

Audit the Wait. Have you been waiting for wisdom—or hiding in fear? Be precise about the difference.

____

____

____

Name the Door. Where do you sense opportunity pressing against your hesitation right now?

____

____

____

Identify the Illusion. What story are you telling yourself to justify staying still?

____

____

____

Choose the Step. What is one faithful action you can take without having the full picture?

____

____

____

Set the Date. When will you move—specifically, not someday?

"My Date: __________________"

Take the Shot. Send the email. Submit the application. Make the call. Do it before you feel ready.

"My Action: ____."

CHAPTER TWELVE

When Obedience Looks Like Defiance

"Why are you breaking the tradition of the elders?"—Matthew 15:2

Growing up Guyanese, I was handed a set of rules before I had language to examine them. Not all of them were written down, but I knew they were there—etched into cultural expectation, family rhythm, and the pews where I sat not just on Sundays, but two other days of the week.

They came with smiles and with warnings, but they carried the same message: speak only when spoken to, do not take up too much space, do not contradict authority, do not be too passionate, too opinionated, too visible—too much.

For a Guyanese boy dreaming of a world he had not yet charted, those rules were stifling. They forced me to color inside lines that did not recognize my God-given purpose.

Then there were the silent rules in church spaces: do not question tradition, do not wrestle publicly with your faith, do not let anyone know you are struggling, do not question God. That last one was the ultimate taboo. But these were not commandments from Scripture. They were whispers in the spaces between praise and worship—rules often more concerned with protecting ritual than nurturing relationship.

I thought I had a firm grip on the difference between the rules meant for my survival and the ones I would need to break in order to be free. God has been teaching me that the line between them is not always so clean

Let me be clear about one thing: **Jesus did not sin**. He did not violate the Law of Moses. Scripture is emphatic that He was without sin. And yet, He was labeled a lawbreaker. Why? Because He broke the Pharisees' interpretation of the Law.

When religious leaders layered man-made traditions around God's commands, Jesus stripped those layers back to reveal the spirit beneath the letter. He healed on the Sabbath. He dined with sinners. He spoke with Samaritans. He touched lepers. He turned tables in the temple when worship became a business.

He did all of this while fulfilling—not abolishing—the Law, because beneath it all were compassion, love, and true obedience to God. He exposed the difference between God's commands and human additions. Between obedience and fear-based compliance. Between holiness and habit.

That distinction matters because breaking the wrong rule is rebellion. But breaking the right one is obedience. Sometimes obedience to God means offending those in power. Sometimes obedience to God means disobeying culture.

I know what this costs.

I remember the season when administrative betrayal stopped being an abstraction and became a room I had to sit in. The pressure, when it arrived, was not loud. It did not announce itself as a test of character. Nothing in the room announced itself as corruption—that is often how corruption survives. It presents itself as order. Procedural. Controlled. The kind of pressure that asks for your silence in polished language and arranges the whole thing to look like routine. What was being asked of me was clear, even without being stated: cooperate, absorb it, move on, protect the system, keep your place. I knew, with a clarity I could not soften, that I would have to make a decision I could not take back. This is what that room looked like.

The last meeting was not loud. That is the part I was not prepared for. I had rehearsed for confrontation—raised voices, administrative deflection, for the clean drama of someone finally saying plainly what had been building for months. Instead: language chosen carefully, blame redistributed gently, the whole thing arranged to feel like procedure rather than what it actually was.

The person across from me knew. I watched their face and I could see it—not malice, not even conviction, but discomfort. The particular discomfort of someone doing a thing they know is wrong and have decided to do anyway. They did not look away. That almost made it worse. They held my gaze with the steadiness of someone who had already made peace with the cost and was waiting for me to make peace with mine.

The expectation was not stated. It did not need to be. It was present in everything that was not said—in the careful language, the procedural framing, the implicit offer of peace in exchange for silence. All you have to do is let it go. All you have to do is absorb it. This is how systems protect themselves. Not with force—with the slow, polished pressure of making compliance feel like the reasonable choice.

I said what I needed to say. I was struggling to keep myself composed, yet I said the truth plainly, in the fewest words it required. And then it was over.

I walked back to my desk, taking in the hallways I'd walked many times—hallways where joy had rung out whenever my name was called. I felt the building moving around me—doors opening, voices in conversation at the end of a day—all of it indifferent to what had just shifted in me. I sat down. I did not reach for my phone. I did not open my laptop. I just sat there in the distinct stillness that follows a decision you cannot take back.

It arrived slowly. First as a kind of clarity—the quiet that comes when you stop negotiating with yourself. Then as something heavier. Not regret. Something closer to grief. Grief for the version of this that could have gone differently if the person across that table had been who I needed them to be. Grief for the months I had spent trying to earn a protection that was never going to come. Grief for the position itself, which I had carried faithfully, and which was now over because I had refused to carry something else alongside it.

I looked at the things on my desk. The small accumulation of a working life—notes, a mug, books I was reading. Ordinary objects that had no idea the context around them had just changed.

I had not broken. That surprised me. I had expected the decision to feel like collapse. Instead, it felt like the opposite—like something that had been pressing against my chest for months had finally been named and released. The cost was real. I knew the cost was real. But the cost of the alternative had always been higher. I had simply been afraid to admit that until there was no room left to avoid it.

I stayed at the desk a little longer than I needed to. Not because there was anything left to do. Because I wanted to be the kind of person who did not run from the room they had just changed. Who let the stillness be what it was—not a defeat, and not yet a victory. Just the first moment of a life that would now have to be built differently. Then I gathered what was mine, and I left.

And I knew, with a clarity I could not soften, that compliance would have cost me more than consequence did. I could feel, even in the aftermath, the shape of the split that had opened in me in that room: one version of myself staying quiet, keeping the position, preserving the appearance of peace. The other telling the truth and accepting whatever came with it. I would like to say the decision felt brave. It did not. It felt expensive. It felt lonely. It felt like choosing to be misunderstood on purpose. But I also knew that if I had agreed to silence in that moment, I would have had to live with the sound of that silence in myself long after everyone else had moved on.

So, I refused to let compliance mute conviction. I refused the kind of peace that depends on pretending. And while I paid a price for it, that price was not my destruction. It was the beginning of my freedom.

Holy defiance is not recklessness. It is obedience to a higher law.

Other biblical examples help me understand when a rule is meant to be broken. Peter and John were ordered to stop preaching. Their response was simple: *"We must obey God rather than men."* Daniel—my namesake—was thrown into the lion's den for praying to God instead of bowing to the decree of a king. Esther went before the king unsummoned, an act punishable by death, to save her people.

None of them were rebels for rebellion's sake. All of them were obedient to a law higher than the one being enforced. This is not a license to do whatever you want under the banner of authenticity. Not every rule is a cage. Some are boundaries that keep us safe, honest, and humble.

Discernment is the difference between breaking rules for ego and breaking them for integrity—between disruption that serves the self and obedience that serves God. Between being disruptive and being destructive.

The real work is asking: **What am I willing to break in order to stay whole in Christ?**

If a rule demands silence in the face of injustice, it needs to break.

If a rule protects image over truth, it needs to break.

If a rule asks me to betray a Spirit-led conviction, it needs to break.

Because I was made to worship in spirit and in truth.

Not every rebel is righteous, and not every sanctuary is a cage. But every righteous person will, at some point, be called to resist corruption, hypocrisy, silence, oppression, and even the version of themselves defined by fear. But never God.

Some rules were never holy to begin with. The hardest part is not identifying which ones. It is finding the courage to stop pretending they are.

What This Season Left Me

The administrative betrayal cost me a job and handed me a question I had been circling for years: What am I willing to lose to stay whole? I learned that holy defiance is not the loud kind. It is quiet, expensive, and almost always private. Nobody claps for it. The freedom it produces is not dramatic either. It arrives slowly, in the ordinary days after the crisis has passed, when you realize you are still standing and still yourself. That is the only proof that matters.

Windowsill Reflections

- Which rules in your life have gone unexamined?
- Where has obedience become avoidance?
- What tradition are you afraid to question—and why?
- What might faithfulness require of you now?

Benediction

May you have the wisdom to honor what gives life, the courage to release what no longer does, and the clarity to obey God even when obedience looks like rebellion.

Running the Play

Name One Rule You Have Followed Out of Fear. Is it "Don't speak up"? "Don't outshine"?

____

____

____

Ask What It Has Protected. Has it kept you safe or just kept you small?

____

Discern the Cost. What price are you paying to keep this peace?

Choose One Faithful Step. How can you loosen its grip this week without burning everything down?

Name the Higher Loyalty. What truth, value, or conviction are you protecting by taking this step?

CHAPTER THIRTEEN

Who Carried Me

"Whoever isolates himself seeks his own desire; he breaks out against all sound judgment."—Proverbs 18:1

Life has a way of aligning the lesson with the season. When I scan the timeline of my life—especially the last nine years—I can say this with certainty: my most vulnerable moments did not happen in failure or loss alone. They happened in isolation. Not solitude. Solitude can be holy. Restorative. Chosen.

Isolation is different. Isolation has a chill to it. A quiet cold that does not announce itself as danger. It wraps around you slowly, like a weighted blanket masquerading as strength. It speaks in phrases that sound resolved, even noble: *"I'm better off alone. I don't need anyone. No one understands anyway."*

But if someone were to press into that mask—really press—they would not find independence. They would find a child. Wounded. Unhealed. Still clutching the lie that isolation is safety and connection is risk.

There was a night in my first year in New York when I received news from home that should have been shared. A loss. The kind that asks to be held by other people. Instead, I sat with it alone for four days, answering messages with *"I'm good"*, filing the grief somewhere I thought was safe.

On the fifth day, I tried to write and found nothing. My emotional reservoir was depleted. Not from overuse, but from under-sharing. I had hoarded the grief the way I had learned to hoard everything: quietly, efficiently, alone. It was only when I finally called someone and admitted what had happened—that the words returned. Not because the grief was gone, but because it was no longer mine alone to carry.

Isolation does not always look like rebellion. For me, it looked like self-preservation. A quiet refusal to be helped. A hardened posture that mistook self-containment for maturity. Left unchecked, it kept me from the very healing I claimed to be pursuing.

It almost always begins with hurt. The deeper the rejection, the sharper the betrayal, the more likely I retreat. Wall by wall. Vow by vow. I called it independence. But it was not strength. It was protection that never learned how to stand down. And over time, with the wound left unhealed, I gravitated toward spaces that validated my pain rather than challenged it. I ran from the healthy because the healthy asks something: **growth, honesty, vulnerability**. This pattern shows up not only in relationships with people, but in relationship with God.

The first time I withdrew, I was five. I did not understand it then. I only understood the instinct: close off. Steel the heart. Blink away tears. Learn early that silence feels safer than being misunderstood.

That moment became a template—a first lie I carried far longer than I realized. It took decades before I allowed God to trace the root. To slow me down enough to let me see that what I had been calling strength was often survival. And survival, when extended too long, begins to suffocate.

For much of my adult life, I lived alone. Physically, yes—but more than that, internally. I had community around me, but distance within me. At first, the solitude was sacred. Necessary. But slowly, quietly, the line blurred. I could no longer tell where holy stillness ended and self-imposed exile began.

Last year, God did something different. The quiet was no longer for hiding. It was for healing. Not the silence of repression, but the silence of reconstruction. He stripped distractions, performances, and excuses—not to leave me alone, but to prepare me to be placed rightly.

Scripture says God sets the lonely in families. He does not merely comfort isolation; He relocates us out of it. But that relocation requires consent. I had to be willing to come out of hiding.

Looking back now, I can see the people who were there all along. Some seasonal. Some foundational. Some who fed me. Some who housed me. Some who prayed when I had no language left. Some who carried strength I mistook for my own.

I cannot lift myself every time. And sometimes the resilience I credit to myself was actually borrowed—held up by others when I was too tired to notice.

This is not a call to reopen every door or return to every space that wounded you. Community requires discernment. Not every crowd is your people. Not every group is your team. Even an eagle will think he is a chicken if he stays in the wrong flock long enough.

Distance can be holy. Separation can be necessary. But isolation, chosen as identity, becomes a trap.

Two are better than one, Scripture says, because when one falls, the other can help them up. Strength multiplies in shared labor. Healing accelerates in safe presence. Perspective widens when you are no longer alone with your worst thoughts.

Even Jesus did not walk alone.

He could have. He did not need twelve. But He chose them—because the Kingdom is not built by solo heroes, but by bodies, families and teams.

The question I had to stop avoiding was simple: was I willing to sacrifice my isolation? Not my boundaries. Not my discernment. But the lie that I had to carry everything alone. I could be strong by myself. I was not meant to be unstoppable by myself.

What This Season Left Me

The grief I hoarded in that first New York year is still the clearest image I have of what isolation costs. Not the grief itself—grief is appropriate, even necessary. What it cost me was five days of carrying something that was never meant to be carried alone. The words came back when I made the call. That is still the most honest thing I know about community: it does not fix what is broken, but it makes the weight distribute differently. That redistribution is not weakness. It is design.

Windowsill Reflections

- Where did isolation first feel safer than connection?
- What lie have you been rehearsing alone that needs light?
- Who has been holding you up without recognition?
- What would strength look like if it included others?

Benediction

May you have the courage to leave the cold behind, the wisdom to choose your people well, and the humility to let love hold you when strength runs thin. May you possess inner strength without requiring yourself to carry the world alone.

Running the Play

Identify the Mask. Where has isolation disguised itself as independence? Where have you refused help to preserve control?

____

____

____

Name Your People. Who sharpens you, not just soothes you? Who tells you the truth with love?

____

Discern Your Distance. Is your separation protective (boundaries) or avoidant (fear)?

Break the Seal. Take one step toward community this week. Reach out. Show up. Let yourself be seen.

CHAPTER FOURTEEN

What the Wound Taught

"My grace is sufficient for you, for My power is made perfect in weakness."—2 Corinthians 12:9

The summer of 2025 surprised me. On paper, the highlight should have been the logistics: serving as chaperone for my high school basketball team in New York, making sure young men far from home were fed, safe, and accounted for. I shared lessons I have learned since leaving high school and college about discipline, patience, and what it means to carry yourself when no one is watching. But the real gift was quieter.

For the first time since 2019, I spent more than two uninterrupted weeks with my mother, Debbie. She was there not as a visitor, but as herself—still the coach of my old high school team, still steady, still present, thirteen years into the role. Still volunteering. Still shaping lives. That alone stopped me.

I grew up in Guyana. I attended The Bishops' High School. That is where my basketball journey began. What most people do not know is that my mother only entered coaching because my first coach quit. The team was going to fold. If we wanted to keep playing, someone had to step in. So she did.

At five feet tall, with no prior coaching experience, no formal training, and no guarantee of success, Debbie volunteered. No pay. No applause. Just responsibility. I remember her staying up late watching drills on YouTube, learning strategy from scratch, building eight-foot shooting dummies out of chicken wire because she could not afford equipment.

She did not do it because she was qualified. She did it because she was willing. Willingness became her curriculum.

What began as a weakness—knowing nothing about the sport—became one of her greatest strengths and the cornerstone of her legacy.

Thirteen years later—after championships, regional travel, and coaching four teams simultaneously—she remains one of the most respected high school basketball coaches in Guyana. Still unpaid. Still present. Still serving players who were never her obligation. She could have stopped when I graduated. She stayed for every player who came after me.

There is a difference between what the wound offers and what the fumble offers. The fumble is a mistake made in motion—an error of execution, of judgment, of timing. Its gift is information: what to do differently next time.

The wound is different. The wound is not something you did wrong. It is something that was done to you, or something that emerged from the deepest gap between who you are and who you are called to be. Its gift is not information, but formation.

The fumble teaches strategy. **The wound teaches empathy**. You cannot lead people through what you have not been willing to walk through yourself.

My own weaknesses rarely announced themselves clearly. They rarely began as inexperience alone. More often, they rose from regret, shame, guilt, or the quiet exhaustion of trying to hold life together while pretending I was fine. They lived in the places I did not post. In the silence after the laughter. In the moments when strength felt performative and survival felt heavy.

Weakness is magnified and concealed at the same time in the world we inhabit. Social media functions as both a highlight reel and a microscope. I have posted the sunlight in the park without mentioning that depression almost kept me in bed all day. I have reposted humor without naming the emptiness behind the stare. I have presented strength when the only thing I could lift was my hands toward heaven, asking God to intervene.

I have done it across years. I have done it in recent months. I have done it in recent days. Weakness is not rare. It is universal.

External—the applications that go unanswered, the groceries that outpace the paycheck, the sixty hours that still cannot cover the bills.

Internal—decisions I regret, mistakes I hide, shame I carry quietly.

Every form of it is an invitation to soul maintenance, but only if I am honest enough to name it. To sit with it. To ask where it came from and what it is trying to teach me.

The apostle Paul understood this deeply. His words in 2 Corinthians were not poetic abstraction. He wrote them amid relentless affliction. He lived them constrained. He did not deny his weakness; he reframed it. He discovered that God's power does not compete with human strength. It replaces it.

"For when I am weak," Paul wrote, *"then I am strong."*

Even Christ Himself modeled this truth. On the cross, in what appeared to be His weakest moment—crying out, forsaken—came His greatest victory. Love held Him there. Weakness became salvation. Death became defeat. That is the pattern.

Strength that endures is rarely built where you feel capable. It is forged where you feel exposed. Where you have nothing left to prove and nowhere left to hide.

When I asked my mother how she managed to keep coaching all these years—without pay, without guarantees, without recognition—her answer was simple: *"All by the grace of God."* And that is the truth beneath all of this: weakness does not disqualify— positions.

It becomes strength not when concealed, but when submitted. Not when romanticized, but when surrendered to God. Grace fills the gaps. Strength grows where ego releases control.

Weakness is not the end of the story. It is often the beginning.

What This Season Left Me

Debbie's chicken-wire shooting dummies are the image I return to most from this chapter. Not the championships. Not the thirteen years. The chicken wire. She built training equipment out of necessity because she had nothing else. What she had was willingness, and willingness, held long enough, became legacy. I have spent more years than I should like to admit trying to enter rooms I was qualified for before I was formed enough to sustain what those rooms required. My mother taught me— not in speech, but in decades of unpaid Tuesday practices—that the gap is not the problem. Despising the gap is.

Windowsill Reflections

- Where have you mistaken weakness for failure?
- What part of your story are you afraid to let God use?
- How might surrender change what you've been trying to control?
- Who are you becoming through this weakness—not despite it?

Benediction

May you find courage in your vulnerability, strength in your surrender, and grace sufficient for every gap you carry. May what once felt like limitation become the place where God's power rests most fully—and may your life testify, not to your resilience, but to His faithfulness. All by the grace of God.

Running the Play

Name the Weakness. What part of yourself have you been hiding, minimizing, or resenting?

Remove the Shame. How has shame distorted your understanding of this weakness?

Invite God In. What would it look like to surrender this area instead of managing it?

Integrate, Don't Erase. How might this weakness refine your leadership, empathy, or discernment?

CHAPTER FIFTEEN

When Safe Became a Cage

"Are you not much more valuable than they?"—Matthew 6:26

I have sat in that room. Not once—several times. The specific kind of silence that fills a conference room when the truth has entered and everyone is terrified to acknowledge it. A decision is being made that violates integrity, ignores justice, or simply insults common sense. I have looked around tables like that. Seen the hesitation in colleagues' eyes. The quick glances downward. Heard the mental calculus in real time: If I speak up, I lose political capital. If I push back, I lose my promotion. If I stand firm, I lose my seat.

I have also been that silence. I have held back in my work, in relationships, even in my walk with God. Choosing safety over surrender. Clinging to the known. I told myself I was being wise. Often, I was simply being afraid.

Security is one of the deepest idols I have carried.

We are taught from a young age to protect the seat, secure the bag, keep the peace. Employment becomes not just a contract for labor, but the source of survival itself. And when your paycheck becomes your provider, your boss becomes your god. I know that tension from the inside. You cannot serve two masters—but most of us spend years trying.

If you had asked me two years ago whether I would complete four poetry books in ten months, I would have laughed. Not because I would not have believed you, but because it was not in my plans. Many are the plans in a person's heart, but it is the Lord's purpose that prevails. What once felt like the ladder being kicked out from under me has been transformed into an elevator, lifting me faster toward purpose.

I am not arguing for recklessness. If you have a job, work it faithfully.

Whatever you do, work at it with all your heart, as working for the Lord, not for human masters. Diligence is not the idol. The idol is the belief that the job is the source.

The difference between working faithfully and worshipping your position is simple: what are you willing to compromise to keep it? What I have learned is that comfort is dangerous.

It kept me stagnant and taught me to trade growth for familiarity—in a role with no real future, in a relationship where the support felt more like sand on a dream than water for it, in a community where my voice was tolerated but never truly heard.

Every time I let go, God proved faithful. Sometimes, though, He had to throw me out in order for me to release my grip. *"See, I am doing a new thing! Now it springs up; do you not perceive it?"* I could not step into my next assignment while clinging to the last one. I could not pick up what was waiting with hands still full of what was.

We understand this instinctively in other areas. We pack old clothes before buying new ones. Fields are burned before they are replanted. But with our lives, we hoard the old season, terrified of the empty space. This is not just my story. It is the pattern of Scripture.

Abraham had to leave his father's house. Joseph was betrayed, forgotten, and left in prison before he was remembered in Pharaoh's palace. Peter had to drop his nets—the very work that fed him—in order to follow Jesus.

Again and again, destiny required departure. Purpose required release. So I have learned not to be afraid of getting fired. A leader who can be bought with a paycheck is not a leader. He is a mercenary. Hold your position loosely so you can hold your integrity tightly.

Do not panic if the ladder gets kicked out from under you. Ladders only get you so far. Elevators rise higher, faster, and to floors you never imagined you would step onto.

If God frees you from the room, it may be because where He is taking you is greater—exceedingly, abundantly greater.

What This Season Left Me

The bad decision gets ratified and everyone keeps their job but loses a piece of their soul. I have been in that room, and I have been that silence. What I know now that I did not know then is that silence compounds. Each time you choose the seat over your conscience, the next choice becomes easier to rationalize. The cost is not always sudden. It is usually gradual—a slow trade of conviction for comfort until one day you realize you have been building in someone else's direction for years. The ladder metaphor only works if you notice early enough that it is leaning against the wrong wall.

Windowsill Reflections

- Is your silence in meetings wisdom, or is it the idolatry of safety?
- What part of yourself are you currently selling to keep the peace?
- Where is God trying to move you while you are still gripping the doorframe?
- Do you trust God enough to catch you if you stand for Him?

Benediction

May you work with excellence, serve with humility, and speak with a boldness that confuses the fearful. May you value your soul more than your seat, and may you always choose dignity over comfort.

Running the Play

Define Your Non-Negotiables. Write down the lines you will not cross. (I will not lie for a client. I will not mistreat a subordinate.)

Audit Your Fear. Who actually signs your checks? Babylon cuts the paper, but Heaven provides the resource.

Declaration:

My provider is _________________.

Prepare the Exit. If you lost this title tomorrow, who would you be? If the answer is no one, you are already in danger.

Loosen Your Grip. What are you holding onto because it feels safe, even though it is shrinking you?

CHAPTER SIXTEEN

After the Drop

"Do not gloat over me, my enemy! Though I have fallen, I will rise."
—Micah 7:8

There are mistakes I can laugh about now. Childhood ones. Teenage ones. A few from my twenties that, with enough distance, have softened into stories instead of scars. But there are others—more recent—that still require conscious release. Choices from the last two years that remind me I am still learning. Still human. Still in need of grace.

Letting go is rarely as simple as I make it sound. I repeat the phrases because they comfort me: Don't cry over spilled milk. Let go and let God. Everything happened the way it was supposed to. And sometimes they help—just enough to get me through the day.

But in private, I replay the moment. I put on a song and spiral. I call someone I trust and circle the same regret again. Or I sit alone and rehearse the scene, especially when the distance between what I wanted and what I got was created by my own hands. Mistakes carry a particular weight when I feel responsible for them.

What I have learned is that collapse is rarely caused by one dramatic decision. It is usually a series of smaller yeses—each one slightly misaligned, each one rationalized. A yes to something I knew better than to accept. Another yes to something I knew would cost me later. And before long, the consequences arrive fully formed, and I tell myself: *"I've already come this far. I might as well see it through."*

Sometimes I catch myself in time. Sometimes I do not. Sometimes I walk away bruised. Other times the fracture remains—relationships altered, trust thinned, years rerouted. There are mistakes I can apologize for. And others I can only integrate.

There is a moment I return to when I want to be honest about what my standards actually cost. A moment with an ex of mine.

We were coming home from a game. My team—Manchester United. I do not remember the game itself—whether we won or lost, what the score was, what happened on the field. What I remember is that I was in my head on the way out. The specific kind of inward that happens when something you care about has not gone the way you needed it to, and you have not yet found the language for what you are carrying.

She asked about buying weed on the way home. It was not the first time she had asked. It was something we had shared—one of the threads of ease in the relationship, the kind of small ritual that signals *we are comfortable with each other, we belong to the same world.* She was not asking anything unreasonable. She was reaching toward the version of us that was easy.

I responded with a venom that surprised even me.

I heard it come out and I did not stop it. Some part of me knew, even in the moment, that what I was saying had almost nothing to do with the question she had asked. What it had to do with was something I had not said aloud to her or to myself: that I wanted her to come back home with me and stay. That I could feel the relationship pulling in two directions. That when I imagined life, I did not want the version of us that involved smoking—I wanted something that felt like a future, and I could not locate the words to explain the difference, so instead the feeling came out as anger aimed at the question she had just asked.

She went quiet.

We walked to and then got on the LIRR. Thirty minutes. I said nothing. Not because I had nothing to say—because everything I had to say was still tangled somewhere below language, and I did not trust myself to reach into it without making things worse. I told myself this was restraint. I told myself I was being careful.

What I was actually being was absent.

We argued when we got in. I do not remember the specific words—they have the quality of things said past the point where words are still the point. What I remember is what she said that landed: *"I don't feel wanted or welcome."*

Not *you were cruel.* Not *you hurt me.* Just that. The quietest possible accusation and the truest one. She did not feel wanted. And she was right. Not because I did not want her—I did. But I had not shown it in any of the ways that would have let her feel it. I had been present in the room for months and absent in the ways that matter. I had been the version of myself that manages rather than opens. That calculates rather than reaches. That stays quiet when the quiet costs someone else something it was not mine to take.

She needed me to communicate. I could not explain everything I was feeling. I was in a fragile place—more fragile than I had admitted to her or to myself—and fragility, for me, had always produced one response: close the door, go somewhere unreachable, wait until I could present a version of myself that was coherent and controlled.

She left that night. We did not speak for a few days. We broke up a week later.

Sometime after that argument—not only because of it, but because of the question it tore open—I quit smoking. I had looked at myself in that exchange and not recognized what I saw. The venom. The silence on the train. The way my inability to explain myself had been received by someone who loved me as proof she was unwanted. I did not know who I was anymore. I knew I needed to change.

And in the quiet that followed, with everything stripped back—the relationship, the habit, the version of myself I had been performing—I felt something I had been keeping at a manageable distance begin to close in. Not as threat but as invitation. I found myself moving toward God in ways I had been circling for years without committing. And in that movement, the writing came.

That is what standards exceeding maturity looks like. Not cruelty. Not anger raised in full knowledge of its damage. Just a man who wanted the right things and could not yet make himself do the right things—in a room, on a train, and at a door she finally stopped knocking on.

That work, ninety poems over thirty-two days—the trilogy that became *Embers of Light and Shadows*—was not produced from mastery. It was born from surrender. I laid down the need to be right, the pressure to be perfect, the instinct to defend myself.

Through that process, God kept returning me to the same truth: **A mistake does not make you unworthy of love**, **grace**, **or a new chapter**.

The fumble is what I did. The wound is what was done to me, or what grew from the gap. The fumble calls for correction and continuation. The wound calls for surrender and formation. The grace of the fumble is not that it did not matter. It did. The grace is that the story is still being written by Someone whose pen is not defined by the worst paragraph.

Mistakes sting. They carry consequences—some temporary, some lasting. But they are not identity. I am not the sum of my worst decisions. I am not the tally of my failures. I am the man whose story is still being written by the One who has never once put down His pen.

Out of that season came a poem—one that sits at the fault line between anger and restraint, between impulse and wisdom. I called it *The Courage Not To*. It was not written to justify silence or spiritualize avoidance. It was written to honor discipline—the kind that chooses peace when destruction would be easier, the kind that corrects without combusting.

That poem taught me something I could not have learned any other way: Growth does not come from erasing mistakes. It comes from integrating them. From asking what they reveal, not only what they ruin.

Scripture has never hidden human failure. It tells the truth plainly. David's choices cost Uriah his life and fractured his household—yet after repentance, he was still called a man after God's own heart. Peter denied Jesus at the moment courage was required most and was later restored, not dismissed. Paul persecuted the very people he would one day shepherd.

None of their mistakes were minimized. But none of them were allowed to have the final word. Grace did. And grace does not mean emotions get a free pass. I have learned this too—the hard way.

Think of the dashboard of a car. The warning lights matter. The signals matter. A check-engine light tells you something is wrong under the hood. Low fuel alerts you to vulnerability. But no one confuses the dashboard for the steering wheel. Those lights were never designed to take control of direction.

Emotions function the same way. They signal. They warn. They reveal. But when they begin to decide—when they grab the wheel—discernment is usually the first casualty.

I have had seasons where anger felt like fuel, pushing me harder on the court, in the gym, in conversation. It gave me intensity and edge. But anger burns fast. When the adrenaline drained, all that remained was exhaustion—bone-deep fatigue that no victory could compensate for.

I have also had moments where sadness or shame convinced me to walk away from opportunities God Himself had placed in front of me. Looking back, those choices did not reflect who I actually was. They reflected who I was in one clouded moment.

And then there is exuberance—the emotion that rarely gets questioned. The joy that loosens restraint. The confidence that spends money you do not yet have. My mother has a phrase for that: *"Eating fowl today, feather tomorrow."* The joy was real. So was the bill. That is the pattern I am learning to live inside of.

I will not pretend the shame disappears overnight. Some memories still whisper accusation. But slowly, steadily, God is teaching me that identity is not forged in what I broke. It is formed in how I rise, how I repent, how I correct course, and how I continue. Grace is not permission to repeat the harm. It is power to change direction.

Mistakes are inevitable. They are part of being human, part of choosing, part of living with agency. But they do not get to name me. They can inform me. They can humble me. They can refine me. They can even become testimony.

But they do not define me.

Correction is not condemnation. Responsibility is not self-hatred. Repentance is not rehearsal of shame. It is release into motion. I am not what went wrong. I am what I am becoming.

What This Season Left Me

The ninety poems in thirty-two days were not a feat of productivity. They were a record of surrender. Each one was a yes to something I had been saying no to—the need to be right, the instinct to defend, the rehearsal of shame. What I understand now about the fumble is that its gift is not comfort. It is not the assurance that everything will be fine. It is the slow, unglamorous work of integration: sitting with what I broke, understanding why, and deciding that the story still has more pages. The pen has not been put down. That is enough to continue.

Windowsill Reflections

• Where have you mistaken regret for identity?
• What lesson are you avoiding by replaying the shame?
• How would your life change if you believed God's grace had the final word?
• What does "continue" look like for you right now?

Benediction

May you release the weight of what went wrong, accept the wisdom it offered, and move forward without dragging yesterday behind you. May you be corrected but not crushed, refined but not reduced. And may you continue—not because you were flawless, but because grace is still writing your story.

Running the Play

I. On the Fumble

Rewrite the Narrative. Choose one mistake you still define yourself by. Write it as a lesson, not a label.

____

____

____

Separate Guilt from Growth. What responsibility belongs to you—and what shame have you added unnecessarily?

____

____

____

Integrate the Insight. What did this mistake teach you that success never could?

____

____

____

Move Forward Cleanly. What does correction look like now—not penance, but progress?

____

____

____

II. On the Signal

Name the Signal. What emotion are you feeling—and what is it pointing to beneath the surface?

____

____

____

Insert the Pause. Where can you create space before responding? (Check HALT: Hungry, Angry, Lonely, Tired?)

____

____

____

Consult Truth. What does wisdom, Scripture, or counsel say beyond how this feels?

____

____

____

Act Cleanly. Choose the response you'll still respect tomorrow.

____

____

____

PART III
LEGACY

Stewardship. Generosity. Permanence:
How do you leave the room better than you found it?

CHAPTER SEVENTEEN

What Was Placed in My Hands

"Continue to work out your salvation with fear and trembling, for it is God who works in you to will and to act in order to fulfill his good purpose."
— Philippians 2:12–13

I tend to see the glass half full—sometimes to the annoyance of the people around me. But even optimists have seasons when the glass looks cracked, leaking, or simply empty. I have known those seasons. Moments when I saw only obstacles instead of openings. Moments when I stayed still even while knowing—deep down—that God was calling me forward. And in those moments, I kept returning to a sentence that refused to let me hide: *"Everything depends on you."*

At first, that phrase sounded naïve, even arrogant. What do I mean? I cannot control the job market. I cannot control other people. I cannot control half the things that happen to me. That is true. But I can control what I believe. I can control how I respond when pressure mounts. I can control whether I remain a passenger in my own life or take responsibility for the wheel. That distinction is the heart of stewardship.

The last two years have been the hardest of my life. They were also the most productive. In the crucible of exhaustion, grief, and uncertainty, I wrote what I now recognize as a life's work of poetry—more than 230 poems across six books. None of it came from comfort. All of it came from staying.

One poem from that season still steadies me when I am tempted to drift. It is called *The Ones Who Stay*. It is about returning—again and again—to unfinished work. About showing up when no one is watching. About holding the roofline steady so others can breathe beneath it. That poem was not aspirational. It was confessional. Because the truth is, there were long stretches when I did not want to stay.

In March 2025, I weighed 166 pounds—physically depleted, emotionally unraveling. The year before had been marked by toxic work environments, verbal abuse, delayed plans, broken trust, and a slow erosion of spirit.

From August 2023 to June 2024, I worked under leadership that fractured my sense of stability. What followed was worse.

There was a night in the middle of a shift working at a restaurant when something broke that I had been holding carefully for months. It did not start as a confrontation. It started as the ordinary friction of a difficult workplace—a disagreement, a decision, something that in a functioning environment would have been handled in a back office in five minutes and forgotten. But this was not a functioning environment. And what followed was not five minutes.

The supervisor came after me through the restaurant. Not pulled me aside. Came after me—through the floor, past tables, past my staff, past guests—screaming. The words were aimed to diminish, to destabilize, to make me small enough to manage. I do not remember every word. I remember the shape of it. The way volume becomes a weapon when someone has decided that your composure is the problem. The way public humiliation is designed to work—to make you either break or retaliate, so that whatever happens next can be made to look like your fault.

I said one thing, repeated: *"I'm trying to leave."*

Not because I had nothing else to say. Because I had too much, and none of it belonged in that room, in front of those people, in that moment. Every lesson I had ever learned about restraint and dignity compressed itself into those four words and held.

Then the phone call came. The owner—family of the supervisor, which explained everything about how this place had always worked—calling to finish what the screaming had started. A different instrument, same purpose. The tone was not controlled this time, it was more inflammatory, the kind of tone that is its own form of contempt. Words chosen to cut along the grain of a man's sense of himself. Designed to make me feel like I was the disruption, the liability, the problem that needed to be managed.

I listened. And then I said: *"I can leave and go home."*

A pause. Then: *"Do that."*

I punched out.

My staff were still on the floor. They had seen the whole thing—the screaming, the phone, the exit. They had kept working through it because that is what staff do, because the room must keep moving even when something is falling apart inside it. But they watched me now with the particular attention of people who have witnessed something and are waiting to understand what it means.

One of them asked if I was coming back. I told them I didn't know. That was the truest thing I had said all night. Not a performance of uncertainty. Actual uncertainty—the kind that arrives when two things are equally real at the same time. I knew what I was walking away from. I did not yet know what I was walking toward. The grief was for the months already spent, for the staff I had come to care about, for the version of this season that had been much harder than it needed to be. The relief was quieter than I expected. Not triumphant. Just the specific relief of a body that has been carrying something heavy and has finally been allowed to put it down. I had been carrying all year up to that point.

I walked out into the night. Streetlights humming steadily as muffled music came through the door. The city did not notice. The street was doing what streets do—movement, noise, people with their own weights going in their own directions. I stood at the bus stop for a moment in the stillness that follows a decision that cannot be undone, and I let both things be true at the same time: that this had cost me something real, and that staying would have cost me more.

I did not know then that this was the bottom. That from this point the only direction available was reconstruction. I only knew that I had said what needed to be said, had not broken in the saying of it, and had left with myself intact. That, for that night, was enough.

From November through March, I disappeared into myself—withdrawn, depressed, spiritually disconnected.

It felt like silence. Like abandonment. But rock bottom has a way of clarifying truth. I realized something painfully simple: no one was coming to rescue me from myself. **God had not abandoned me**—but I had abdicated responsibility for my own life. I had outsourced agency to circumstance. I had mistaken waiting for faithfulness.

Stewardship begins where excuses end. And once excuses end, influence begins. I could remain seated in despair, or I could move. So I moved. I recommitted—fully, without performance, without pretense. I returned to the gym. I returned to prayer. I returned to discipline. One choice at a time. Slowly, strength came back. Clarity returned. Faith became practiced again, not merely imagined.

That is when I understood what everything depends on you really means. It does not mean you are your own savior. It means God will not steer a vessel that refuses to move.

Stewardship is the willingness to take responsibility for what has been entrusted to you—your body, your gifts, your influence, your choices—especially when no one is applauding. Leadership begins long before anyone follows you. It begins the moment you decide to stop being passive with your own life.

I have closed doors on myself and justified it with language that sounded wise: *"It is not the right time, I need more clarity, I'm waiting on God."* But often, what I was really doing was avoiding accountability because growth was asking too much. Freedom of choice does not mean freedom from consequence. Many of the conditions I have lived in are the result not of what I chose, but of what I refused to choose. Sometimes, the greatest trespasser against my own future has been me.

Accepting responsibility for your own life is where stewardship begins—

but it does not end there. Because once you accept that responsibility, you inevitably become responsible for others, whether you want to or not. People are watching how you carry what you have been given. You are either building or neglecting. You are either guarding what has been entrusted or allowing it to erode.

Pain may not be your fault. But healing will always depend on what you do next.

As my pastor Richard Ishmael often says, ***"In the midst of crisis, we are focused on who Christ is."*** That focus—where you look, what you believe, what you choose to act on—is yours to steward. Not because you are sufficient, but because responsibility is often the doorway through which grace enters.

What This Season Left Me

One hundred sixty-six pounds is the most specific number in this book. I did not put it here because it is dramatic. I put it here because it is true. The weight was a record of what those two years had cost. Coming back from it was not one decision. It was the decision to make the next decision, and then the next. The gym came before the clarity. The prayer came before the peace. None of it arrived in the order I expected, and none of it arrived because I waited for conditions to improve. Stewardship is not a feeling. It is a return—to the work, to the practice, to the life you are called to carry—one choice at a time.

Windowsill Reflections

• Where are you calling delay obedience?
• What responsibility are you avoiding because it feels heavy?
• Who benefits if you stay passive?
• What would change if you acted like your choices mattered—because they do?

Benediction

May you carry what has been entrusted to you with courage and clarity. May you stop waiting for rescue and start practicing stewardship. May God meet you in motion, strengthen you in obedience, and shape your life—choice by choice—into something that can bear weight. May you lead first by how you live.

Running the Play

Identify the Drift. What area of your life are you currently leaving to chance or circumstance?

____

____

____

Name the Choice. What decision are you avoiding that would move you forward?

____

____

____

Remove the Excuse. What justification sounds wise but keeps you stuck?

____

____

____

Act Today. Choose one concrete step that proves you are no longer a passenger.

____

____

____

Connect the Thread. Look back at what you named under "Identify the Drift." Now look at what you committed to under "Act Today." Write one sentence that makes those two things the same story.

"I was drifting in ___________________________________ and today I

am choosing ___________________________________ as my first

act of stewardship.

____

____

CHAPTER EIGHTEEN

The Lines I Drew

"Do not conform to the pattern of this world, but be transformed by the renewing of your mind."—Romans 12:2

The clearest picture I have of what life looks like without a governing code is a season I spent in reactive mode—months when every decision was made in response to what had just happened rather than in alignment with where I was going.

Someone would challenge me and I would spend three days formulating a response. An opportunity would arrive and I would spend two weeks deciding whether to take it, because there was no internal system that could evaluate it quickly. A setback would come and I had no language for what it meant, no framework to place it in, no governing principle that could absorb the hit without buckling.

A code is not a comfort. It is infrastructure. And without it, you are at the mercy of whatever the most recent input was. Whether I had named it or not, I was already living by a code—just not one I had chosen. Every life is shaped by rules: some inherited, some absorbed, some chosen, many never examined. The danger is not that we lack rules. The danger is that we outsource them.

We live in a culture of constant input—news cycles, social feeds, private conversations, public outrage, humor used as anesthesia—everything competing for attention. Slowly, almost imperceptibly, what we consume becomes what we contemplate. What we contemplate becomes what we believe. And what we believe becomes the architecture of our lives.

Our feeds reveal what we value. Our conversations expose what we rehearse. Our circles reflect what we have normalized. The question is not whether your thinking is being shaped. The question is by whom.

The average mind produces far more thoughts than it can faithfully govern. That alone explains why clarity is rare and overwhelm is common—especially for those of us who spend more time alone with our thoughts than we once did.

But the more pressing question is not the volume. It is this: how many of those thoughts are constructive? How many are corrosive? How many are even yours?

It is not difficult to understand why pessimism thrives. The world is loud with fracture. Cynicism feels sophisticated. Hope is often mislabeled as denial. We even have language for it now—toxic positivity—as if believing in redemption is somehow naïve. But Scripture never asks us to pretend pain does not exist. It asks us to refuse to let pain have the final word.

There is a difference between ignoring reality and disciplining attention. When Paul writes, *"Whatever is true, whatever is noble, whatever is right, whatever is pure...think on these things,"* he is not prescribing blind optimism. He is calling for mental governance. This is not mood management. This is command-center control. Because thought is never neutral.

It is always moving—either toward formation or deformation. Left untrained, the mind does what it has always done: loops fear, rehearses failure, narrates worst-case futures, and mistakes repetition for truth.

I know this terrain intimately. I have shared openly about seasons where my thinking isolated me—where spirals convinced me to withdraw from people who loved me, to accept narratives that felt familiar but were false. The damage was not immediate. It was cumulative. Thought by thought, belief hardened into behavior.

As Scripture says, as a man thinks, so is he. Thoughts are seeds. Whatever you water will grow. Water bitterness, and resentment takes root. Water envy, and comparison chokes joy. Water defeat, and momentum dies quietly. But water gratitude, and perspective shifts. Water faith, and endurance strengthens. Water truth, and peace stabilizes even in chaos.

This kind of mental discipline does not happen accidentally. It requires training. We understand this instinctively with the body: repetition builds muscle, discipline compounds strength, and no one expects physical transformation without intention. The mind is no different.

This past year, as much time as I spent rebuilding my body, I spent confronting my thinking. When the thought arrived—*"I'll never get there"*—I learned to answer it: ***"I'm already on the way."*** When doubt screamed—*"You've failed too many times"*—I responded with evidence: ***"I've learned too much to quit now."*** And when fear whispered—*"You're not enough"*—I answered with truth: ***"Christ in me is more than enough."***

This is not self-hypnosis. It is allegiance. The enemy does not need to destroy a life if he can first distract the mind. A distracted person is disarmed, and a disarmed person cannot fight. That is why Scripture frames transformation as cognitive before it is behavioral. *"Be transformed by the renewing of your mind."*

Renewal precedes obedience.

Belief precedes action.

Code precedes conduct.

Before I could lead others, I had to define what governed me. Before I could inherit responsibility, I had to clarify conviction. Not more motivation—a governing code. Rules are not restrictive when they are chosen. They are protective.

That code is not borrowed from culture, not inherited from fear, not shaped by my worst day. It is forged through truth, experience, and faith. It determines which thoughts are entertained and which are escorted out. It decides what narratives get airtime and which ones get challenged. It tells the mind where authority lives.

And it is not a one-time draft. Codes are written, tested, revised. What mattered at twenty may not serve at forty. Wisdom refines what survival once demanded. But the responsibility remains: Govern your thinking, or it will govern you.

What This Season Left Me

The three thought-counterarguments in this chapter—I'll never get there. You've failed too many times. You're not enough—were not written for a book. They were written in the dark, on the days when the spiral was louder than any other voice in the room. What I know now is that the practice of answering the thought is not about optimism. It is about refusing to let an unchallenged lie become a governing belief. The mind will produce the thought regardless. The code is what determines whether that thought gets to stay.

Windowsill Reflections

- What thoughts dominate your quiet moments?
- Which narratives feel familiar but may not be true?
- Who benefits if you remain mentally undisciplined?
- What would change if your thinking obeyed conviction instead of mood?

Benediction

May you become a faithful steward of your mind. May you govern your thoughts with courage and clarity. May you live by conviction, not impulse—by truth, not noise. And as you write your code, may it steady you, shape you, and prepare you for the responsibility that comes next.

Running the Play

Audit Inputs. What are you feeding your mind daily—news, conversations, entertainment, silence? Adjust accordingly.

Find the Root Belief. Before you write your code, identify what is generating the loop. For the negative thought you named, complete this sentence:

"This thought keeps returning because somewhere I believe

Now ask: is that belief true, partially true, or a lie that once protected you?

It is:

That answer is what your code is actually governing. Write the code now.

Draft the Code. Write 3–5 personal rules that govern how you think under pressure.

Interrupt the Loop. When a familiar negative thought appears, write its counter-truth immediately.

The Lie:

____

____

____

The Truth:

____

____

____

Revisit Weekly. A code only works if it is lived. Revise as wisdom grows.

____

____

____

Connect the Thread. Your code is only as strong as the moment it costs you something. Looking back at Chapter 17—the drift you named, the choice you avoided—write one rule from your code that directly addresses that pattern.

"The rule I need most right now is

____

because it speaks directly to _______________________________

118

____

______________________________________."

CHAPTER NINETEEN

Bring Your Own Ball

"For we are God's handiwork, created in Christ Jesus to do good works, which God prepared in advance for us to do."
—Ephesians 2:10

There was a Thursday night in October 2025 that quietly clarified something I had been learning for years. I returned to the St. John's President's Dinner—an annual event I knew well. In 2019, I had sat in that ballroom as a student member of the President's Society, working the room, learning the language of proximity and possibility. This time, I entered as a *Graduate of the Last Decade* and as CEO of Turning Words Into Windows LLC. I was no longer assisting the vision. I was carrying one.

The moment was not loud. It was grounding. A reminder of distance traveled—and of how often progress begins without permission. Not bad for a boy from Guyana who arrived here bright-eyed and uncertain, holding little more than an idea and the will to steward it.

Bring your own ball.

As children, we all learn this lesson early. Games of cricket, basketball, or football end abruptly when the person who owns the ball has to leave. Play stops—not because the desire is gone, but because the equipment is. After enough disappointing endings, the logic becomes clear: if you brought your own ball, the game could continue. Someone had to go? Fine. You would keep playing. The pace was yours. The time was yours.

As adults, we pretend the playground disappeared. It did not. The arena just changed. We are still playing—building careers, communities, callings. But many of us are still waiting for someone else to supply the ball: the funding, the invitation, the platform, the permission. We say when I have, as though readiness is something bestowed rather than built.

Stewardship establishes responsibility. Governing the mind determines direction. Initiation is where both become visible. And once something becomes visible, it carries weight beyond you.

I learned this not in theory, but in transition.

My arenas have shifted often—from basketball courts to classrooms, from libraries to boardrooms. I once split zone defenses on the hardwood; later, I split different ones in classrooms at All Hallows in the Bronx. Up top were negative self-talk and disbelief. Down low were fear, circumstance, and pride. The ball was no longer leather and air. It was content, care, and conviction, placed into the hands of students who needed to believe again.

And when that arena changed suddenly—when leadership faltered and doors closed—I stopped waiting for a whistle. I looked at what was already in my hands and began to build.

Turning Words Into Windows® was not a miracle at first. It was obedience. A pen. A story. A voice. A willingness to initiate without applause. There were years before I brought my own ball when I was very good at waiting in line. I had talent—I knew that—but I kept it in reserve, holding it back until the right invitation arrived, until someone with more authority than me confirmed that I was ready for the room.

I volunteered when others led. I contributed when others initiated. I was present, but passive. And I confused presence with participation.

The cost of that was invisible for a long time. Only later, when I stopped waiting and started building, did I realize how many seasons I had spent standing at the edge of my own potential, watching others play the game I had come to play.

Scripture confirms the pattern. Moses hesitated at the call to lead. God did not hand him something new; He asked a revealing question: *"What is in your hand?"* Moses answered honestly: a staff—ordinary, worn, familiar. Yet that same staff parted seas and struck water from rock.

The widow in 2 Kings believed she had nothing except a little oil. That oil, once surrendered, paid every debt and preserved her family. The boy in John 6 offered five loaves and two fish. To the disciples, it was insufficient. In Jesus' hands, it fed thousands.

The pattern is consistent: God works with what is already present. He does not bless comparison. He blesses commitment.

What I have learned is not about accumulating more before beginning. It is about honoring what is already present—gifts, skills, experience, empathy, discipline, insight. Whatever is in the hand is the ball.

When I kept waiting for someone else to supply the game, I was always subject to when they decided to leave the court. But when I initiated with what I carried, the game did not end when others walked away. It simply moved arenas.

Sometimes God removes you from a space not to punish you, but to reveal that what you thought was small was actually sufficient all along—a staff, a jar of oil, a lunch, a calling.

What This Season Left Me

The St. John's President's Dinner is one of the few moments in this book where I name a date, a room, and a year. I do that deliberately. Distance traveled is easier to deny when it stays abstract. Walking back into a room you once sat in as a student—this time carrying a title you built—is the kind of evidence that does not permit romanticization. Progress happened. Not because the invitation was extended. Because I stopped waiting for it.

Windowsill Reflections

- What are you waiting to be given that you already possess in seed form?
- Where have you mistaken smallness for insufficiency?
- What would change if you initiated without asking permission?
- Who benefits if you bring your own ball to the game?

Benediction

May you arrive equipped. May you stop despising what looks small and start stewarding what is already yours. May you initiate with courage, build with faithfulness, and trust that the God who placed it in your hands knows exactly what He intends to do with it.

Running the Play

Take Inventory—With Evidence. Do not list what you wish you had. List only what you have already used. Complete each line.

"In the last 90 days, without anyone's permission, I

____."

"In the last 90 days, without anyone's permission, I

____."

"In the last 90 days, without anyone's permission, I

____."

Those three things are your ball. Everything else is what you are growing toward.

Start Small. Choose one action this month that uses what is already in your hand.

____

____

Handle Rejection Cleanly. Initiation invites resistance. Do not let it re-define you. How will you respond when the first door doesn't open?

____

____

____

Keep Playing. When one arena closes, move the game. Do not stop. What is your next arena?

____

____

____

Connect the Thread. The drift you named in Chapter 17 and the code you wrote in Chapter 18 both assumed you were waiting for something. What you just inventoried proves you were not. Write one sentence that closes that gap.

"I already had _______________________________ and did not treat it

as enough because ____

____."

CHAPTER TWENTY

The Weight of One Day:
The 24-Hour Rule

"Enlarge the place of your tent, stretch your tent curtains wide, do not hold back; lengthen your cords, strengthen your stakes."—Isaiah 54:2

"Therefore do not worry about tomorrow, for tomorrow will worry about itself. Each day has enough trouble of its own."—Matthew 6:34

I.

When I returned to poetry at the end of 2022, two phrases began echoing through my work—phrases I did not yet realize were diagnosing my life: certain uncertainty and comfort tested against growth's rubric.

They first appeared in *Reflections: A Journey Within* as confessions. The future felt unformed. Plans were provisional. But beneath the surface, something more than challenge was happening. Something was being widened

There is a law in construction that applies equally to the soul: you cannot build a skyscraper on a bungalow foundation. If you want to go higher, you must first go wider. And widening is painful. It requires breaking existing concrete in order to pour something deeper.

Comfort is a container. It has a specific volume. It holds exactly what you currently have—your current skills, your current patience, your current income, your current influence.

If you pray for more—more opportunity, more impact, more connection—but refuse to stretch the container, the prayer cannot be answered in full. Not because God is withholding, but because there is no room. If He poured more into a full life right now, it would spill. It would be wasted. Or worse, it would shatter the container entirely. Growth's rubric is the

124

measurement of that container.

It asks a harder question than most of us want to answer: Can you hold the weight of what you are asking for?

During my master's program, this reality was relentless. Over two years, I taught more than two hundred students across ten classes. I planned lessons on trains. I graded papers between stops. Some nights I wrote until two in the morning, slept a few hours, and returned to teach before eight.

At the time, I thought I was just grinding. I now realize I was strengthening my stakes. God was not punishing me with exhaustion. He was expanding my threshold for pressure. He was teaching me how to function when the conditions were not perfect. He was widening the tent so that, years later, when I had to lead a company, manage a brand, and steward a community, I would not collapse under the weight. He was protecting my future by inconveniencing my present.

This is why this belongs in the Legacy section. If this were just about you, staying small would be fine. A small tent is perfectly adequate for one person. It is cozy. It is safe. But legacy is about shelter. It is about building something large enough for other people to stand under.

Stretch your patience so you can mentor a difficult employee without snapping. Stretch your finances so you can fund a vision that outlives you. Stretch your emotional intelligence so you can navigate a marriage through a storm. Your capacity becomes the ceiling for everyone following you. If you refuse to grow, the people you lead will eventually hit your lid.

The test is not: **Are you happy?**

The test is: **Are you expanding?**

When the stretching comes—when the schedule tightens, when the demand increases, when impostor syndrome flares—do not pray only for the pressure to stop. Do not ask only for a lighter load. Pray also for a stronger back. That pressure is the tent peg being driven further out. It hurts because you are becoming larger. Do not resent the stretch. You are being prepared to hold the harvest.

But expansion brings its own temptation. When your life starts widening, your mind often widens with it in the wrong way. You begin trying to carry everything at once—what happened yesterday, what is due today, what might go wrong tomorrow. I know that temptation well. There were seasons when my responsibilities were growing, but my inner life had not yet learned proportion. My schedule expanded faster than my peace. I was becoming capable in public while becoming crowded within.

That is where the second discipline became necessary.

II.

The same God who stretches the tent does not ask you to carry the whole harvest before it arrives. Expansion is the long work. But inside the long work, there is a daily mercy: living within the grace of one day.

There is a particular kind of exhaustion that comes from trying to live in three tenses at once—regretting yesterday, managing today, fearing tomorrow. The mind stretches thin trying to hold the past, the present, and the future in a single grasp. But we were designed to inhabit only one moment at a time. Any attempt to live outside of today produces anxiety.

I learned this the hard way. When I was teaching, writing, and surviving toxic environments all at once, my mind was constantly racing ahead. *What if this contract ends? What if the money runs out? What if I made the wrong choice three months ago?* I was physically present but mentally time-traveling.

And because I was never fully in the room, I missed the grace available for that specific day. I was trying to solve next month's problems with today's strength. The math never works.

God gives manna for the day. He does not give manna for the month. If you try to hoard grace for the future, it rots. If you try to borrow it from the past, it is stale.

This is why I established the 24-Hour Rule for myself. It is a boundary for the soul. It forces me to close the tab on yesterday and refuse to open the tab on tomorrow before I have actually lived today.

The rule works in two directions: victory and defeat.

In victory, when the book launches, the game is won, the praise arrives—there are twenty-four hours to celebrate. Soak it in. Feel the joy. Be grateful. But when the clock turns, move on. If you stay in the celebration too long, confidence curdles into arrogance. You begin to believe you have arrived, and you stop doing the work that got you there. Yesterday's home runs do not win today's games.

In defeat, when the rejection comes, the mistake happens, the relationship ends—there are twenty-four hours to grieve. Feel the sting. Cry. Write the angry letter and burn it. Sit in the disappointment. But when the clock turns, move on. If you stay in the grief too long, disappointment hardens into bitterness. You start identifying as a victim rather than a learner.

The 24-Hour Rule is a reset button. It acknowledges that life is a series of days, not one continuous emotional event. It allows full humanity—the highs and the lows—without permitting either one to become an identity.

This, too, is about capacity. You cannot solve a lifetime of problems in a single afternoon.

When the anxiety of the future presses in, I ask myself a simple question: **Can I do anything about this in the next twenty-four hours?** If the answer is yes, I do it. If the answer is no, I release it. Worrying about a problem you cannot solve today is like revving a car in neutral—you burn gas, but you go nowhere.

There is a profound freedom in shrinking your horizon. When the mountain looks too high, do not stare at the summit. Look at your feet. Take the step available to you today. Then do it again tomorrow. Endurance is just a series of twenty-four-hour cycles strung together.

What This Season Left Me

The tent stretches over years. The manna falls one morning at a time. Both are true, and they are not in conflict. I have spent seasons trying to live too far ahead of my actual grace, reaching for tomorrow before I had fully inhabited today. What I am learning now is that expansion requires patience, and peace requires proportion. God calls me to endure the long widening and to live the day I have actually been given.

Windowsill Reflections

• Is your current life a ceiling or a floor for the people coming after you?
• What blessing would actually overwhelm you right now because you lack the structure to hold it?
• Where have you mistaken growing pains for failure?
• What past victory are you still relying on for today's confidence?
• What past failure are you still punishing yourself for?
• How much energy are you spending on problems that don't belong to today?

Benediction

May you be willing to be widened. May you value capacity more than comfort. May you accept the mercy of the sunrise and release the weight of the sunset. May you live fully in the day you have been given, trusting that tomorrow has its own grace waiting—and that you are being made large enough to hold it.

Running the Play

Part I—Expand the Tent

Audit the Container. Look at the thing you are praying for—the job, the relationship, the platform. Now look at your current habits. If God gave it to you today, would it crush you?

Strengthen the Stakes. Pick one area where your capacity is weak.

Spiritual: Can you sit in silence for 20 minutes?

Mental: Can you read a difficult book without checking your phone?

Emotional: Can you receive criticism without spiraling?

Area of Weakness:

Plan to Strengthen:

Name the Stretch. The next time you feel stretched thin, do not ask only, *Why is this hard?* Ask, *What is this season enlarging in me?* What is being widened in you right now?

Build for More Than Yourself. Who will be better served, protected, or strengthened if your capacity grows in this area?

____

____

____

Bridge the Two Halves. Capacity is built across years. Peace is practiced across days. Before moving to the 24-Hour Rule, connect them.

Name one area where you are currently being stretched (from Part I):

____

Now name the one daily worry about that area that you cannot resolve in the next 24 hours:

____

Cross it out. The stretch is long work. Today's assignment is not to finish it. Today's assignment is:

____

Part II—The 24-Hour Rule

Set the Clock. When a major event happens—good or bad—acknowledge the clock.

"I have until _________________ tomorrow to dwell on this."

Audit the Worry. List your current anxieties. Circle the ones you can impact in the next 24 hours. Cross out the rest.

____

____

____

Choose Today's Assignment. What is the one thing that actually requires your attention in the next twenty-four hours?

____

____

____

Close the Day. Create a nightly ritual that signifies done. A prayer, a journal entry, closing the laptop.

My Closing Ritual: _______________________________________

____

____

Reset the Morning. Start every day at 0-0. No carrying over yesterday's score. What do you need to release before tomorrow begins?

____

____

Connect the Thread. You have now named the stretch being built in you and identified the worry that doesn't belong to today, and chosen today's assignment. Put those three things into one sentence.

"I am being enlarged in _______________________________. Today's

assignment is _______________________________. And the worry I am

releasing is ____

____."

CHAPTER TWENTY-ONE

Where I Could Finally Stand

"Two are better than one… If either of them falls down, one can help the other up. But pity anyone who falls and has no one to help them up."—Ecclesiastes 4:9–10

There is a reason athletes talk about home court in hushed, reverent tones. It is not just about familiarity. It is about reinforcement. It is about playing in a space that remembers who you are—even on nights when you forget. A place where the walls echo belief, where the floor absorbs impact, where the crowd does not need convincing. Something changes when the ground beneath you is for you.

Earlier in this book, I wrote about the wound of isolation. This chapter is about the answer to that wound: the kind of community that makes it possible to stand again. I was reminded of this at a wedding.

One of my closest friends got married—someone I have known my entire life in New York. Blood could not have made us closer. Standing beside him as he committed himself to his wife, I felt the gravity of something older than romance: endurance. The quiet miracle of two people choosing to walk with each other, season after season. I heard the familiar jokes— *you're next*—and laughed them off. But what stayed with me came later.

At the end of the reception, the newlyweds thanked the people who had carried them: parents, siblings, mentors, childhood friends, coworkers, prayer partners. It was a roll call of witnesses. A public acknowledgment that no life is built alone. I was honored to be named.

But more than that, I was struck by a truth that would not let me go: nobody survives, succeeds, or grows alone. Every life is lifted by the hands that hold it.

From the moment we open our eyes, we are placed into community. At first, it is given to us—family, caregivers, teachers. Later, it becomes chosen: friends who become brothers, teammates who become anchors, coworkers who become confidants, spiritual kin who become pillars. Together, they form something essential: home court.

This is why the loss or disruption of community feels so destabilizing. When the people around you change, the ground shifts. You are no longer supported by what was and not yet rooted in what will be. I lived there for months this year. It was quiet. Lonely. Disorienting. But when I finally paused long enough to take inventory, I realized my community had not vanished. It had evolved.

And that, too, is part of stewardship. Not every supporter is meant to stay for every season. Some people walk with you through construction. Others through maintenance. Others through demolition. Letting go does not always mean betrayal. Sometimes it is alignment. Sometimes love looks like prayer from a distance. That is still community.

When I look back honestly, every major season of growth in my life was marked not only by God's presence, but by people. People who saw me when I was unclear. Who corrected me when I was drifting. Who prayed when I could not find the words. Who loved me back to myself when I forgot who I was. I was never as alone as my doubt insisted.

That is the essence of home court advantage: voices that lift instead of drain, presence that steadies instead of distracts, belief that reinforces what God is already doing.

We glamorize independence in this culture. We wear *self-made* like a badge of honor. But isolation is one of the enemy's most effective strategies. I was never designed to win by myself. Even Jesus did not do it that way.

He had the Multitude—those He ministered to publicly, who received His teaching but did not know His interior. He had the Twelve—a chosen community who lived alongside Him, saw His humanity, and carried His mission. He had the Three—the innermost circle, the ones who witnessed His anguish and His glory. He knew exactly who belonged in which circle. He did not cast His pearls to the multitude, and He did not hide His heart from the three.

The mistake is not having the wrong people in our lives. The mistake is confusing access with intimacy—giving public people private authority, and inviting those who only know your image to speak into what is still sacred.

But here is the tension we rarely admit: we want community without vulnerability. We want support without exposure. We want affirmation without correction. That is not home court. That is an audience. Building a true home court required letting people see me. Letting them speak into me. Real home court advantage is not an echo chamber where everyone applauds. It is a place where you are safe enough to be challenged.

A true teammate will say when your form is off. They will say when you are acting out of ego. They will say when the story you are telling yourself is no longer true. Iron sharpens iron, and sharpening always requires friction.

A community does not need to be large. It needs to be true. Two or three people to call at midnight. A few voices that can tell the truth without trying to control you. People who hold space for who you are becoming— not who you were performing as.

There was a season when God was nudging me back toward community. Back toward friends I had drifted from. Back toward spaces I had abandoned when life became loud. Back toward Him. Because how can I claim independence from the One who created me?

Scripture is unambiguous: God places the lonely in families. Burdens are meant to be shared. Presence multiplies strength. Community is God's strategy for both protection and purpose.

Building a home court is a responsibility—not with everyone, but with the right ones. The people who reinforce the calling rather than compete with it. The people who make obedience feel possible, not lonely.

The calling may be individual. The journey is not.

What This Season Left Me

The roll call of witnesses at that wedding was not really about the newlyweds. It was about the people who had shown up, season after season, before anyone was watching. That is the picture I carry of community: not the celebration, but the years before it. The friends who stayed when I was unclear. Who prayed when I had no words. Who loved me back to myself. I was named in that roll call not because I was present that night, but because I had been present through the years that made the night possible. That is what home court means. You show up before you are needed so you are there when it matters.

Windowsill Reflections

- Who knows your real story—and still stands with you?
- Are you confusing an audience (applause) with a home court (support)?
- Who has permission to tell you when you are wrong?
- Who needs you to be home court for them?

Benediction

May you build ground that holds you. May you choose people who sharpen, not scatter you. May your environment reinforce your obedience, your joy, and your becoming. And may you never forget: you were not meant to run your race alone.

Running the Play

Audit the Court. Draw three circles (The Multitude, The Twelve, The Three). Place the people in your life into the correct circles. Are you giving 'Three' access to 'Multitude' people?

Draw here:

Adjust One Circle. For each person currently in the wrong circle, name the one adjustment—not a confrontation, not a conversation, just a change in the level of access you grant—that would place them correctly.

Person: _________________ Currently in _____________________________

Should be in: _______________________.

Adjustment: ____.

Person: _________________ Currently in _____________________________

Should be in: _______________________.

Adjustment: ____.

Person: _________________ Currently in _______________

Should be in: ____________________________.

Adjustment: ____.

Do not announce the adjustment. Simply make it.

Name The Gap. Where in your life are you asking for support while resisting vulnerability?

____

____

____

Strengthen the Court. Who is the one person you need to reconnect with, thank, or invite into deeper trust this week?

____

____

____

Be Someone's Home Court. Who around you needs reinforcement, not advice? Reach out with presence, prayer, or practical support.

____

____

____

Connect the Thread. Look back at the code you drafted in Chapter 18. Is there a rule in that code that you have only been able to keep because of someone in your Three circle? Name them and name the rule.

"_____________________________ has made it possible for me to keep the

rule: ____

____."

Have you told them? Yes / No

If no—that is this week's act of home court.

CHAPTER TWENTY-TWO

The Hallway Between Doors

"For the revelation awaits an appointed time; it speaks of the end and will not prove false. Though it linger, wait for it; it will certainly come and not delay."—Habakkuk 2:3

We love the testimony of the open door. We celebrate the breakthrough, the arrival, the yes. But we rarely talk about the hallway. The space between the door that closed behind you and the one that has not yet opened in front of you. The hallway is quiet. It is dim. And it is almost always longer than we expected.

In a culture of instant gratification, delay feels like failure. If it has not happened yet, we assume something is wrong. *"Maybe I heard God wrong. Maybe I am being punished. Maybe I missed my window."*

But in the economy of the Kingdom, delay is often a tool of development. God is rarely in a rush. He is far more interested in who you are becoming than in how quickly you arrive. He knows that if He opens the door before you are ready, the weight of the blessing may crush you. So sometimes He keeps you in the hallway.

There is a difference between holy waiting and fearful stalling, and the season itself will not always tell you which one it is.

Holy waiting is active. It has direction even when it has no timeline. It moves, prays, prepares, develops—just without the door yet.

Fearful stalling wears the language of waiting, but it is rooted in avoidance. You are not in the hallway because God placed you there. You are in the hallway because you have been afraid to knock.

The diagnostic I use is simple: *"Does this waiting feel like preparation or like hiding? Am I building capacity for what is next, or preserving comfort by calling inertia patience?"*

God is not opposed to waiting. He is opposed to the kind of self-deception that pretends we are waiting on Him when we are actually waiting on ourselves.

I have spent years in the hallway. Waiting for the visa. Waiting for the degree. Waiting for the career to align. Waiting for the promise to manifest. There were days I kicked the doors. Days I slid down the wall in despair. But looking back, I realize the hallway was where the real work happened.

In the hallway, I learned to pray when I did not feel like it. In the hallway, I stripped away the idols of performance and applause. In the hallway, I learned that my identity is not attached to a room. It is attached to God.

Delay exposes motives. *"Why do I want the door to open? Is it for His glory, or for my validation?"* If I cannot worship in the hallway, I will not worship in the room. I will just worship the room.

There is also a difference between a **No** and a **Not Yet**. A No is a redirection. A Not Yet is a preparation. Discernment is knowing the difference. If the dream remains alive in the spirit even when the circumstances are dead, it may not be over. It may simply be waiting for its appointed time.

Hold on.

But waiting is not passive. Many people treat the hallway like a waiting room. They sit, read magazines, zone out. Active waiting looks different. It sharpens skills. It deepens character. It serves where it is. The hallway is not a timeout. It is a training ground.

Joseph waited thirteen years between the dream and the palace. David waited years between the anointing and the crown. Jesus lived thirty years before His public ministry began.

Do not despise the timeline.

When the door finally opens—and it will, if it is meant to—I believe I will be grateful for the time spent in the hallway. The delay did not deny the blessing. It built the character necessary to keep it.

What This Season Left Me

The hallway is where I met God outside of performance. Not on a stage. Not in a role. Not with anything to prove. Just me, the quiet, and the question of whether I believed what I said I believed. The answer was sometimes yes, sometimes no, and sometimes I was too tired to know. What I can say is this: I did not leave the hallway the same person who entered it. The visa, the degree, the career, the promise—those were the doors. The hallway was the formation. I would not trade it, though I would not wish it

Windowsill Reflections

- What door are you banging on that God has told you to wait for?
- How has your character grown during this season of delay?
- Are you ready for the weight of what you are asking for?
- Can you trust God's timing more than your deadline?

Benediction

May you find peace in the pause. May you trust the silence of the hallway. May you wait with active hope, knowing that the God who promised is faithful to perform what He has spoken.

Running the Play

Name the Hallway. What area of your life feels stuck right now?

____

____

Shift the Question. Instead of asking "When?", ask "What?" What is this season trying to teach me?

Active Waiting. Choose one skill or habit to develop while you wait. Prepare for the room you want to enter.

Preparation or Hiding—Produce the Evidence. The hallway is only holy if you are building inside it. Answer both columns honestly.

What I am actively doing while I wait:

What I am avoiding under the name of waiting:

Now answer plainly: is this holy waiting or fearful stalling?

It is: ____

If it is holy waiting: what is the one thing you will build this week inside the hallway?

If it is fearful stalling: what is the one move you have been calling patience?

Connect the Thread. The 24-Hour Rule from Chapter 20 applies here too. Name one worry about the closed door that does not belong to today.

Cross it out. Name what today's hallway assignment actually is.

CHAPTER TWENTY-THREE

Guard What Guards You

"Above all else, guard your heart, for everything you do flows from it."
—*Proverbs 4:23*

In sports, the locker room is a sacred space. It is the one place where the cameras are not allowed. Where the fans cannot see. Where the performance stops. In the locker room, a player can be injured. Can be tired. Can be frustrated. Can be real. It is where the team bonds, where the strategy is built, and where the truth is told.

If the locker room is compromised—if leaks happen, if trust is broken, if outsiders are let in—the team eventually falls apart on the field. There is no winning public battles without private safety.

A life has three spaces.

The Arena: the public space—work, social media, performance, the version of you that everyone sees.

The Lobby: the semi-private space—acquaintances, casual friends, the extended network; some access, but limited.

The Locker Room: the inner sanctum—the heart, the home, the closest confidants, the relationship with God.

The mistake many of us make is giving Arena people Locker Room access.

We let strangers' opinions dictate our self-worth. We share our deepest dreams with people who have not earned the right to hear them. We let the noise of the world invade the quiet of our spirit.

I have made this mistake.

There was a season when I was sharing the manuscript of my first book while it was still in draft—still tender, still close to the bone. I handed pieces of it to people who had access to me, but not relationship with me. They were around. They were available. They were easy to send it to. But they had not carried any of the cost of the work. They had not sat with the story long enough to know what it meant to place those pages in their hands.

I remember waiting for their responses with more hope than wisdom. A text notification would appear, and I would reach for my phone as though affirmation might steady the vulnerability of having been seen. But what came back was thin, distracted, or casual. Sometimes a short reaction. Sometimes a delayed one. Sometimes comments that treated what was sacred to me as though it were merely content to skim between obligations.

Nothing they said was devastating on its face. That was almost the worst part. The wound was not dramatic enough to justify itself publicly. But I could feel something in me folding inward. What had felt alive on the page suddenly felt exposed. Not wrong, not even bad—just mishandled. I had offered tenderness where there had only been proximity. I had given Lobby people Locker Room access to something that was still learning how to stand.

And for months after that, I felt the effect. I second-guessed lines that had once felt true. I grew quieter around the work. I became more hesitant with the very thing I had been called to make. The manuscript had not changed. But the atmosphere around it had. What deflated was not the calling. It was my sense of safety around it.

That experience taught me something I should have learned earlier: access and intimacy are not the same thing. Availability is not covenant. Just because someone can reach you does not mean they are qualified to hold what is most fragile in you.

The lesson was not to stop sharing. The lesson was to become discerning about with whom and when. Protecting the locker room is not secrecy. It is sanctity.

Boundaries are not walls. They are gates. They determine what gets in, what stays out, and what has to wait. Without guarding the locker room, there is eventually nothing left to give in the arena.

Protecting the locker room means guarding peace—understanding that not every crisis deserves your adrenaline. It means guarding the ear—being careful who you listen to and whose voice is allowed to carry weight in you.

It means guarding rest—recognizing that you cannot be "on" around the clock and still remain whole. And it means guarding intimacy—marriage, family, friendship, the walk with God. These are not for public consumption.

I have seen leaders collapse because they had no locker room. They lived entirely in the arena. They performed until they hollowed out. There has to be a place where a person does not have to be "on." A place where they are loved not for what they produce, but for who they are.

This also means removing people who violate the room. If someone leaks your confidence, minimizes your pain, or brings toxicity into your sanctuary, they lose their access card. That is not cruelty. That is stewardship. The team cannot be protected if the room is not protected. The heart works the same way.

What guards you must also be guarded. Peace is not passive. Trust is not automatic. Access is not owed. The inner life needs protection because everything public is downstream from everything private. If the sanctuary is breached, the strain eventually shows up in the game.

That is why discernment matters so much. Not everyone who claps for you belongs near your core. Not everyone who is curious about your life is safe enough to hold it. And not every relationship that began with access deserves to keep it.

The locker room is not locked because love is scarce. It is guarded because what lives there is sacred.

What This Season Left Me

I did not understand proximity without covenant until I felt the cost of it. People can be physically near—in your inbox, at your table, reading your draft—and still be strangers to the work. The manuscript deflating in me was not ultimately their fault. They could not have known how tender it was, because I had not required them to know me before I gave them access. Sanctity is not about walls. It is about stewardship. The locker room is not sealed shut. It has a door. And the door has a standard.

Windowsill Reflections

- Who is in your Locker Room that drains you instead of refilling you?
- Where are you letting public opinion influence private peace?
- Do you have a space where you can be completely unmasked?
- What needs to be evicted from your heart today?

Benediction

May you guard your heart with diligence. May your sanctuary be safe and your rest be deep. May you know the difference between who watches you and who is with you.

Running the Play

Audit the Access. List the names of people who currently have Locker Room access. For each one ask honestly: have they earned it? If not, identify which circle they actually belong in.

____

____

____

Name the Cost Already Paid. Before you adjust who has access going forward, account for what unguarded access has already cost you. This is not self-condemnation. It is accurate record-keeping.

"Because I gave _______________________________ Locker Room access

before they earned it, I lost or diminished _______________________________

____."

"What I know now that I did not know then is _______________________________

____

____."

That knowledge is the new standard. Write it into your code from Chapter 18 if it is not already there.

Close the Gate. Identify one person or input (news, social media) that needs to be moved from the Locker Room to the Lobby. Do not announce it. Simply stop granting that level of access.

____

____

Create the Sanctuary. Designate a physical space or time where "Arena" talk (work, stress) is not allowed. Protect it like a contract.

My Sanctuary:

____

Rebuild One Wall. What boundary have you let erode that needs to be restored this week?

____

____

____

Connect the Thread. The Three circle you audited in Chapter 21 and the Locker Room you are guarding now should be the same group of people. Are they?

My Three Circle and my Locker Room are: the same / different (circle one.)

If different, name who needs to move and in which direction:

____

CHAPTER TWENTY-FOUR

The Inheritance

"A good man leaves an inheritance for his children's children"
—Proverbs 13:22

In sports, you never really own the jersey. You rent it. The number on your back was worn by someone before you, and it will be worn by someone after you. The job is not to keep it forever. The job is to play in a way that adds value to the number—to leave behind a standard of excellence, integrity, and effort so that the next person who puts it on feels the weight of what came before them.

Life is a borrowed jersey. Position, influence, resources, even breath—entrusted for a season. The question is not *"What can I get?"* The deeper question is *"What will I leave?"*

That is the shift from success to significance. Success is about what you accumulate. Significance is about what you distribute. Success is about a name. Significance is about the Name above every name.

For a long time, I thought legacy was something you built at the end of your life—a building, a scholarship, a will. I understand now that legacy is what you are building every day. It is the culture you create in your home. It is the way you treat the barista. It is the words you write that will be read when you are gone. It is the investments you make in people who can do nothing for you in return.

The moment this became personal for me happened not at a milestone, but at a funeral. I sat in a room listening to people describe a man whose name I will not write here, and what struck me was not the tributes to what he had accomplished. It was the testimony of what he had made possible in other people.

His legacy was not a list of achievements. It was a room full of people living differently because he had poured himself into them without keeping score. On my way home that night, one question would not let me go: If I left tomorrow, what room would gather? What would be said? Not about the books I intended to write, or the degrees I earned, or the titles I held. About the way I had loved people. About whether anyone was stronger, freer, steadier because I had been here. I did not have a satisfying answer. That was the beginning of taking legacy seriously.

There are two ways to live: as a cul-de-sac, where everything comes and stops—hoarding resources, knowledge, and credit until the flow ends with you. Or as a conduit, where what comes to you also moves through you—receiving to release, learning to teach, earning to give. The Kingdom is built on conduits. Freely you have received; freely give. He who refreshes others will himself be refreshed.

I want to leave a jersey that is heavy with glory. I want my students to stand on my shoulders. I want my children to start their race halfway down the track because of the ground I took. I want to make it easier for the next dreamer from Guyana, the next writer, the next believer, the next person trying to build a life from faith and fragments.

And when I think about what that kind of inheritance looks like in lived form, I think of Debbie. Long before I had language for legacy, she was teaching me that what gets passed down is not only money or opportunity, but steadiness, sacrifice, discipline, and care. Some of what I hope to leave in others was first practiced in front of me by someone who kept showing up without asking to be praised for it.

That kind of inheritance requires a death to ego. It means planting trees under whose shade you will never sit. It means caring more about the future than about immediate credit. It means living with the end in mind.

We are all ancestors in training. The inheritance being stored up is not just money. It is emotional health, spiritual fortitude, and patterns of faithfulness. Healing trauma leaves a legacy of wholeness. Breaking the cycle of addiction leaves a legacy of freedom. Walking with God leaves a map for those coming after you.

The jersey is on loan. It gets worn well. Played hard in. Sweated through. Then given back. The only question worth asking is whether it will be worth wearing when the next person puts it on.

What This Season Left Me

I drove home from that funeral asking a question I could not answer, about a man whose name I will not write, in a room I did not expect to change me. What struck me most was not that he had been extraordinary. It was that he had been consistent. He had poured into people without keeping score for long enough that a room full of them gathered to say so. That is not a dramatic act. It is a daily one. Legacy is not a monument. It is a practice. I am still learning it.

Windowsill Reflections

• Are you building a kingdom for yourself or for others?
• What generational cycle are you called to break?
• Who are you mentoring?
• If you left your position today, would the next person be set up for success or cleanup?

Benediction

May you live with open hands. May you build more than you consume. May your ceiling become the next generation's floor. And when you finally take off the jersey, may it be worn, stained with effort, and heavy with glory.

Running the Play

Identify the Heir. Who is coming after you (in work, family, ministry)? Are you preparing them?

____

____

Open the Hand. What resource—knowledge, money, connection—are you hoarding that needs to be shared?

____

____

____

Break the Cycle. What negative pattern stops with you so it doesn't pass to the next generation?

____

____

____

Draw the Thread. Before you write the sentence you want said about you, look back across Part III and complete this account. This is the foundation the eulogy rests on.

From Chapter 17—the drift I named and chose to steward:

____

From Chapter 18—the rule from my code I most need to keep:

____

From Chapter 19—the thing already in my hand that I will steward:

____

From Chapter 21—the person in my Three circle without whom none of this holds:

____

From Chapter 23—what am I now guarding so the inheritance is not compromised:

____

Now write the eulogy sentence. It should be able to carry all five of those answers inside it.

"My sentence:

____

____."

The Eulogy Test. The sentence above is what your journey built. The sentence below is what you are committing to live. Write one sentence you want said about you when you are gone. Live that sentence today.

My Sentence:

____

____

____

The Last Play. You have now run the plays across eight chapters of Part III—and across the entire playbook. Before you close this book, name one thing you will do differently this week because of what you built here. Not a resolution. Not a vision. A specific, dateable action.

Action: ____

Date: _______________________   Time: ____________________

Who will know: ____

The playbook is only paper until that moment. That moment is where it becomes yours.

EPILOGUE

The Final Whistle

"For He knows our frame; He remembers that we are dust."
—Psalm 103:14

Today, as I write this, winter wind moves through the trees outside my window, bending leafless branches in a slow choreography. My apartment is quiet. Suki and Lucy are asleep in their beds, fully surrendered to whatever dream-world cats inherit. There is no crowd here. No scoreboard. No visible audience for the final chapter.

Just me at my desk. A blinking cursor. And the dawning awareness that I have written my way through twenty-four chapters across a year that stretched me beyond what I thought I could hold: growth sharpened by pain, by endings I did not want, by beginnings I did not see coming.

Behind these chapters sit six books of poetry. There are classrooms I once sat in quietly, then returned to years later as a guest speaker. There are games: some buzzer-beaters, some blowouts, some I did not survive in overtime. There are heartbreaks and hellos. Breakthroughs and prayers whispered through tears that spilled like ink across blank pages. Nights with smoke in my lungs, ice in my cup, and whiskey trying to treat loneliness like it was a cold.

Through it all, one truth kept rising: None of this started with me. None of this will end with me.

I am not the coach. I am not the owner of the court. I am a player entrusted with a jersey and a set of plays, invited into a game already in motion long before I laced my shoes or drew my first breath.

That is where this lands: **remember whose game this is**.

Responsible, yes. In charge, no.

That distinction matters because it is where many of us break. We plan. We carry unfinished work into a new year and stack fresh resolutions beside it. We try again. We tell ourselves that if we get the plays right, the scoreboard will tilt.

I believed that if I trained hard enough, studied long enough, stayed disciplined enough, surely the outcome would match the effort.

That belief held as long as the scoreboard cooperated. But when it did not, when I did the right things and still watched doors close, when I carried integrity and still ended up on the wrong end of injustice, when God felt quiet not because He was absent but because the story was moving in ways I could not map, I realized how addicted I was to understanding.

Somewhere along the way, I had started treating my relationship with God like a franchise I was managing on His behalf. As if everything hinged on my discipline, my precision, my ability to hold it together.

Life proved otherwise. I could not deliver myself in the midnight hour. I could not perform my way into grace. I could not hustle my way into peace. This does not erase responsibility. It clarifies it. Choices matter. Obedience matters. Character matters.

But I did not design the court. I did not write the physics of the ball. I did not manufacture tomorrow. I did not breathe life into my lungs this morning.

And thank God I did not, because if the world sat on my shoulders, the weight would crush me. That is the freedom beneath everything: not powerless, **but not God**.

I sat with that for a long time.

Not the idea of it. I have known the idea for years. What I sat with was the weight of finally meaning it. There is a difference between knowing you are not God and actually putting the franchise down. The first is theology. The second is a Tuesday.

I closed the laptop. Suki and Lucy slept in the living room. Outside, the winter wind still moved through the branches the same way it had when I started this page.

I sat in that quiet for a while. No music. No words. No celebration. Just the stillness that comes when something has been finished and you have not yet filled the space with what comes next. And in that stillness, without trying, I went back.

Not to last year. Not to New York. Back further than that. Back to the crowded departure lounge with wire for windows. Back to the school uniform and the Guyana morning and the airplane ascending.

And further still, back to the bench at the schoolyard gate, where a five-year-old boy sat alone in the lengthening afternoon light, listening for footsteps that would mean he had not been forgotten, deciding quietly that he was fine before anyone arrived to ask.

That is where the question started. Not at the airport. The airport was where someone left. The bench was where he understood what leaving meant and chose to carry it alone rather than let it show.

That choice, made before he had language for it, before he knew it was a choice, is what this book has been the slow undoing of.

From where I stand now, I can finally answer what that boy was really asking. Not *Why do people always leave?* But *Am I worth staying for?*

The answer this book has been building toward is not a guarantee. It is something truer: the people who mattered most did not leave. They became the material of this book. Debbie. The unnamed ones in the acknowledgments. The voices that corrected me, the hands that steadied me, and the communities that absorbed my failures and multiplied my growth.

The airport was not an ending. It was the first page.

And this, this annotated life, written across a month but lived across a decade, is not an ending either. It is a handoff. It is what the boy at the airport eventually had to offer once he stopped waiting to be rescued and started learning how to build.

The whistle has not blown yet. But when it does, I want to have finished the race. Not the way I started it, breathless and afraid and wondering why people leave. I want to finish it the way all good races end: with everything spent, nothing withheld, and a lane that is cleaner for having been run.

Go build something worth inheriting.

Benediction

May you play faithfully. May you steward your gifts with courage and carry your days with humility. May you release what was never yours to control and rest in the hands of the One who holds the whole court. And when the buzzer sounds on this season, may you be able to say: I ran my race. I played my part. I trusted the One who knew the final score long before the tip-off.

GAME FILM

Scriptural Foundations for the 24 Chapters

I have learned that it is Scripture that shows you why the hard-won lessons hold. Throughout this book, I have shared my life and what I have learned from it. Yet none of these chapters were invented by me. They are echoes of a deeper Truth—principles woven into the fabric of the world by the Architect of the game.

Use this section as your film room. Return to it when you need to anchor a season in something stronger than willpower. Meditate on these passages, memorize them, and let them dwell in you richly. The chapters change, the seasons change, but it is the Word which stands forever.

PART I—ORIGINS
Who you had to become before the game began · Chapters 1–8

Chapter One: Eight Christmases

- **2 Timothy 4:7**— "I have fought the good fight, I have finished the race, I have kept the faith."
- **Hebrews 12:1**— "Let us run with perseverance the race marked out for us, fixing our eyes on Jesus."
- **Galatians 6:9**— "Let us not become weary in doing good, for at the proper time we will reap a harvest if we do not give up."
- **Ecclesiastes 7:8**— "The end of a matter is better than its beginning, and patience is better than pride."

- **Philippians 1:6**— "Being confident of this, that he who began a good work in you will carry it on to completion until the day of Christ Jesus."

Chapter Two: The Word I Refused

- **Psalm 19:12**— "But who can discern their own errors? Forgive my hidden faults."
- **Jeremiah 17:9**— "The heart is deceitful above all things and beyond cure. Who can understand it?"
- **Psalm 139:23–24**— "Search me, God, and know my heart; test me and know my anxious thoughts."
- **John 8:32**— "Then you will know the truth, and the truth will set you free."
- **Lamentations 3:40**— "Let us examine our ways and test them, and let us return to the Lord."

Chapter Three: Carry Each Other

- **Ecclesiastes 4:9–10**— "Two are better than one… If either of them falls down, one can help the other up."
- **Galatians 6:2** — "Carry each other's burdens, and in this way you will fulfill the law of Christ."
- **Proverbs 27:17**— "As iron sharpens iron, so one person sharpens another."
- **Romans 12:15**— "Rejoice with those who rejoice; mourn with those who mourn."
- **1 Thessalonians 5:11**— "Therefore encourage one another and build each other up, just as in fact you are doing."

Chapter Four: Pressuh Does Buss Pipe

- **Luke 12:48**— "From everyone who has been given much, much will be demanded; and from the one who has been entrusted with much, much more will be asked."

- **James 1:2–3**— "Consider it pure joy whenever you face trials of many kinds, because you know that the testing of your faith produces perseverance."
- **2 Corinthians 4:8**— "We are hard pressed on every side, but not crushed; perplexed, but not in despair."
- **1 Peter 1:7**— "These have come so that the proven genuineness of your faith—of greater worth than gold—may result in praise, glory and honor."
- **Proverbs 24:10**— "If you falter in a time of trouble, how small is your strength!"

Chapter Five: No One Can Beat Me But Me

- **Luke 14:28**— "Suppose one of you wants to build a tower. Won't you first sit down and estimate the cost to see if you have enough money to complete it?"
- **Mark 8:36**— "What good is it for someone to gain the whole world, yet forfeit their soul?"
- **1 Corinthians 9:25**— "Everyone who competes in the games goes into strict training. They do it to get a crown that will not last, but we do it to get a crown that will last forever."
- **Matthew 16:24**— "Whoever wants to be my disciple must deny themselves and take up their cross and follow me."
- **Proverbs 21:5**— "The plans of the diligent lead to profit as surely as haste leads to poverty."

Chapter Six: The Decimal Difference

- **Proverbs 24:16**— "For though the righteous fall seven times, they rise again."
- **Micah 7:8**— "Do not gloat over me, my enemy! Though I have fallen, I will rise. Though I sit in darkness, the Lord will be my light."
- **Philippians 3:13**— "Forgetting what is behind and straining toward what is ahead."

- **Psalm 37:23–24**— "The Lord makes firm the steps of the one who delights in him; though he may stumble, he will not fall."
- **Romans 8:28**— "And we know that in all things God works for the good of those who love him, who have been called according to his purpose."

Chapter Seven: The J Train

- **1 Corinthians 15:58**— "Therefore, my dear brothers and sisters, stand firm. Let nothing move you."
- **Hebrews 10:23**— "Let us hold unswervingly to the hope we profess, for he who promised is faithful."
- **Ephesians 6:13**— "Therefore put on the full armor of God, so that when the day of evil comes, you may be able to stand your ground."
- **Colossians 2:6–7**— "So then, just as you received Christ Jesus as Lord, continue to live your lives in him, rooted and built up in him."
- **Psalm 119:30**— "I have chosen the way of faithfulness; I have set my heart on your laws."

Chapter Eight: Blending Is Not Becoming

- **1 Samuel 16:7**— "The Lord does not look at the things people look at. People look at the outward appearance, but the Lord looks at the heart."
- **Psalm 139:14**— "I praise you because I am fearfully and wonderfully made; your works are wonderful, I know that full well."
- **Galatians 1:10**— "Am I now trying to win the approval of human beings, or of God? If I were still trying to please people, I would not be a servant of Christ."
- **Luke 16:10**— "Whoever can be trusted with very little can also be trusted with much."
- **Matthew 25:21**— "Well done, good and faithful servant! You have been faithful with a few things; I will put you in charge of many things."

PART II—THE ARENA
What the game demanded · Chapters 9–16

Chapter Nine: What Survives the Crossing

- **Proverbs 17:27**— "The one who has knowledge uses words with restraint, and whoever has understanding is even-tempered."
- **Colossians 4:6**— "Let your conversation be always full of grace, seasoned with salt, so that you may know how to answer everyone."
- **Proverbs 25:11**— "Like apples of gold in settings of silver is a ruling rightly given."
- **James 1:19**— "Everyone should be quick to listen, slow to speak and slow to become angry."
- **Ephesians 4:29**— "Do not let any unwholesome talk come out of your mouths, but only what is helpful for building others up according to their needs."

Chapter Ten: Before You Move

- **Matthew 7:24**—"Everyone who hears these words of mine and puts them into practice is like a wise man who built his house on the rock."
- **1 Peter 1:13**—"Therefore, with minds that are alert and fully sober, set your hope on the grace to be brought to you."
- **Galatians 6:9**— "Let us not become weary in doing good, for at the proper time we will reap a harvest if we do not give up."
- **Ephesians 6:11**—"Put on the full armor of God, so that you can take your stand against the devil's schemes."
- **Luke 14:31**—"Or suppose a king is about to go to war against another king. Won't he first sit down and consider whether he is able?"

Chapter Eleven: When They Counted Me Out

- **1 Timothy 6:12**— "Fight the good fight of the faith. Take hold of the eternal life to which you were called."

- **1 Samuel 17:48**— "As the Philistine moved closer to attack him, David ran quickly toward the battle line to meet him."
- **Ecclesiastes 11:4**— "Whoever watches the wind will not plant; whoever looks at the clouds will not reap."
- **Hebrews 11:1**— "Now faith is confidence in what we hope for and assurance about what we do not see."
- **2 Timothy 1:7**— "For the Spirit God gave us does not make us timid, but gives us power, love and self-discipline."

Chapter Twelve: When Obedience Looks Like Defiance

- **Acts 5:29**— "Peter and the other apostles replied: We must obey God rather than human beings!"
- **Matthew 15:3**— "Jesus replied, "And why do you break the command of God for the sake of your tradition?"
- **Daniel 3:18**— "But even if he does not, we want you to know, Your Majesty, that we will not serve your gods or worship the image of gold you have set up."
- **Galatians 5:1**— "It is for freedom that Christ has set us free. Stand firm, then, and do not let yourselves be burdened again by a yoke of slavery."
- **Romans 12:2**— "Do not conform to the pattern of this world but be transformed by the renewing of your mind."

Chapter Thirteen: Who Carried Me

- **Proverbs 18:1**— "Whoever isolates himself seeks his own desire; he breaks out against all sound judgment."
- **Ecclesiastes 4:12**— "Though one may be overpowered, two can defend themselves. A cord of three strands is not quickly broken."
- **Hebrews 10:25**— "And let us not neglect our meeting together, as some people do, but encourage one another."
- **Proverbs 18:24**— "One who has unreliable friends soon comes to ruin, but there is a friend who sticks closer than a brother."
- **Psalm 68:6**— "God sets the lonely in families."

Chapter Fourteen: What the Wound Taught

- **2 Corinthians 12:9**— "My grace is sufficient for you, for my power is made perfect in weakness."
- **Psalm 34:18**— "The Lord is close to the brokenhearted and saves those who are crushed in spirit."
- **Genesis 50:20**— "You intended to harm me, but God intended it for good to accomplish what is now being done."
- **Psalm 147:3**— "He heals the brokenhearted and binds up their wounds."
- **Isaiah 40:29**— "He gives strength to the weary and increases the power of the weak."

Chapter Fifteen: When Safe Became a Cage

- **Matthew 6:26**— "Look at the birds of the air; they do not sow or reap or store away in barns, and yet your heavenly Father feeds them. Are you not much more valuable than they?"
- **Proverbs 29:25**— "Fear of man will prove to be a snare, but whoever trusts in the Lord is kept safe."
- **Psalm 118:6**— "The Lord is with me; I will not be afraid. What can mere mortals do to me?"
- **Hebrews 13:6**— "So we say with confidence, "The Lord is my helper; I will not be afraid."
- **Isaiah 43:18–19**— "Forget the former things; do not dwell on the past. See, I am doing a new thing!"

Chapter Sixteen: After the Drop

- **Micah 7:8**— "Do not gloat over me, my enemy! Though I have fallen, I will rise."
- **Lamentations 3:22–23**— "Because of the Lord's great love we are not consumed, for his compassions never fail. They are new every morning."
- **Proverbs 24:16**— "For though the righteous fall seven times, they rise again."

- **1 John 1:9**— "If we confess our sins, he is faithful and just and will forgive us our sins and purify us from all unrighteousness."
- **Proverbs 25:28**— "Like a city whose walls are broken through is a person who lacks self-control."

PART III—LEGACY
What you build after the whistle · Chapters 17–24

Chapter Seventeen: What Was Placed in My Hands

- **Philippians 2:12–13**— "Continue to work out your salvation with fear and trembling, for it is God who works in you to will and to act in order to fulfill his good purpose."
- **1 Corinthians 4:2**— "Now it is required that those who have been given a trust must prove faithful."
- **Matthew 25:29**— "For whoever has will be given more, and they will have an abundance."
- **Colossians 3:23**— "Whatever you do, work at it with all your heart, as working for the Lord, not for human masters."
- **1 Peter 4:10**— "Each of you should use whatever gift you have received to serve others, as faithful stewards of God's grace."

Chapter Eighteen: The Lines I Drew

- **Proverbs 23:7**— "For as he thinks in his heart, so is he."
- **Philippians 4:8**— "Finally, brothers and sisters, whatever is true, whatever is noble, whatever is right… think about such things."
- **2 Corinthians 10:5**— "We demolish arguments… and we take captive every thought to make it obedient to Christ."
- **Proverbs 4:23**— "Above all else, guard your heart, for everything you do flows from it."
- **Romans 12:2**— "Do not conform to the pattern of this world, but be transformed by the renewing of your mind."

Chapter Nineteen: Bring Your Own Ball

- **Exodus 4:2**— "Then the Lord said to him, "What is that in your hand?" "A staff," he replied.
- **2 Kings 4:2**— "Elisha replied, "How can I help you? Tell me, what do you have in your house?" "Your servant has nothing there at all, except a small jar of olive oil.""
- **Ecclesiastes 9:10**— "Whatever your hand finds to do, do it with all your might."
- **Judges 6:14**— "Go in the strength you have and save Israel out of Midian's hand. Am I not sending you?"
- **Ephesians 2:10**— "For we are God's handiwork, created in Christ Jesus to do good works, which God prepared in advance for us to do."

Chapter Twenty: The Weight of One Day: The 24-Hour Rule

- **Isaiah 54:2**— "Enlarge the place of your tent, stretch your tent curtains wide, do not hold back; lengthen your cords, strengthen your stakes."
- **James 1:4**— "Let perseverance finish its work so that you may be mature and complete, not lacking anything."
- **Romans 5:3–4**— "We also glory in our sufferings, because we know that suffering produces perseverance; perseverance, character; and character, hope."
- **Matthew 6:34**— "Therefore do not worry about tomorrow, for tomorrow will worry about itself. Each day has enough trouble of its own."
- **Exodus 16:19**— "Then Moses said to them, "No one is to keep any of the manna until morning.""

Chapter Twenty-One: Where I Could Finally Stand

- **Ecclesiastes 4:9–10**— "Two are better than one… If either of them falls down, one can help the other up."

- **Proverbs 13:20**— "Walk with the wise and become wise, for a companion of fools suffers harm."
- **1 Corinthians 15:33**— "Do not be misled: 'Bad company corrupts good character.'"
- **Hebrews 12:1**— "Therefore, since we are surrounded by such a great cloud of witnesses, let us run with perseverance the race marked out for us."
- **Psalm 133:1**— "How good and pleasant it is when God's people live together in unity!"

Chapter Twenty-Two: The Hallway Between Doors

- **Habakkuk 2:3**— "For the revelation awaits an appointed time… Though it linger, wait for it; it will certainly come and will not delay."
- **Isaiah 40:31**— "But those who hope in the Lord will renew their strength. They will soar on wings like eagles."
- **Romans 8:25**— "But if we hope for what we do not yet have, we wait for it patiently."
- **Galatians 6:9**— "Let us not become weary in doing good, for at the proper time we will reap a harvest if we do not give up."
- **Psalm 27:14**— "Wait for the Lord; be strong and take heart and wait for the Lord."

Chapter Twenty-Three: Guard What Guards You

- **Proverbs 4:23**— "Above all else, guard your heart, for everything you do flows from it."
- **Proverbs 25:17**— "Seldom set foot in your neighbor's house— too much of you, and they will hate you."
- **Psalm 91:1**— "Whoever dwells in the shelter of the Most High will rest in the shadow of the Almighty."
- **Matthew 6:6**— "But when you pray, go into your room, close the door and pray to your Father, who is unseen."
- **Matthew 7:6**— "Do not give dogs what is sacred; do not throw your pearls to pigs."

Chapter Twenty-Four: The Inheritance

- **Proverbs 13:22**— "A good person leaves an inheritance for their children's children."
- **Psalm 78:4**— "We will not hide them from their descendants; we will tell the next generation the praiseworthy deeds of the Lord."
- **2 Timothy 2:2**— "And the things you have heard me say in the presence of many witnesses entrust to reliable people who will also be qualified to teach others."
- **Psalm 145:4**— "One generation commends your works to another; they tell of your mighty acts."
- **Deuteronomy 6:6–7**— "These commandments that I give you today are to be on your hearts. Impress them on your children."

Epilogue: The Final Whistle

- **Psalm 103:14**— "For he knows how we are formed, he remembers that we are dust."
- **Proverbs 16:9**— "In their hearts humans plan their course, but the Lord establishes their steps."
- **Psalm 24:1**— "The earth is the Lord's, and everything in it, the world, and all who live in it."
- **Isaiah 55:8–9**— "For my thoughts are not your thoughts, neither are your ways my ways, declares the Lord."
- **Revelation 22:13**— "I am the Alpha and the Omega, the First and the Last, the Beginning and the End."

ACKNOWLEDGMENTS

I did not write this book in my own strength. Even when the writing happened in solitude—late nights, early mornings, quiet apartments, and borrowed tables—there were voices, hands, prayers, and histories holding the work up long before the words arrived on these pages.

First, to God. The Author and Finisher of every good thing in my life. Thank You for the grace You showed me when I tried to play owner instead of steward. For the mercy that met me in my blind spots. For the correction that shaped me, the silence that taught me, and the grace that carried me when I could not carry myself. Every chapter in this book is, at its core, a response to Your faithfulness to me.

To my family by birth and choice—past, present, and remembered. To the generations whose sacrifices I benefit from but did not witness. To the ones who prayed when I didn't have the voice. To those who modeled strength, even when life asked too much of them. I carry you with me in ways I am still learning how to name.

To Debbie and Beverly. Your fingerprints are everywhere in this book, whether your name appears or not. You taught me how to prepare before opportunity arrived, how to honor responsibility, and how to trust God's timing even when it made no sense. You believed in my calling before I had language for it, and you never confused talent with character. Thank you for building a foundation I could stand on long before I knew I would need it.

To Pastor Richard Ishmael and the Church City USA family. You gave me a spiritual home during the most disorienting season of this decade. Pastor Richard, your investment in my character—not just my gifts—has helped shape the man who eventually dared to write this book. Thank you for seeing what God was building before the building was visible, and for lending your voice to these pages.

To my teachers, coaches, mentors, and leaders. The formal and the informal. Those who corrected me when it was uncomfortable. Those who challenged me when it would have been easier to stay quiet. Those who let me fail without abandoning me. You taught me that development is not about applause, but about formation.

To my students. From the day I started teaching, you reminded me why clarity matters, why language shapes futures, and why stewardship is not optional when people are watching how you live. Teaching you sharpened my own thinking, exposed my inconsistencies, and forced me to practice what I claim to believe. You have given me far more than I have given you.

To my friends—both the ones who stayed and the ones who left. The ones who listened without fixing. The ones who told me the truth without trying to control me. The ones who saw me when I was strong and when I was tired, and loved me in both places. You are my home court.

To the communities that shaped me. Guyana, for giving me roots. New York, for continuing to refine me. To the classrooms, gyms, churches, writing rooms, and quiet corners where growth happened slowly, honestly, and unwillingly. Each space left a mark.

To Suki and Lucy. You two have anchored me to the present when my mind wanted to live everywhere else. You reminded me that care, routine, and quiet companionship are also forms of grace.

This book is not a declaration of mastery. Quite the opposite—it is a record of learning. Of falling, adjusting, listening, and getting back in position. May you take what serves you, leave what doesn't, and continue writing a life that reflects integrity, courage, and faith—wherever the game finds you next.

I am eternally grateful.
—Daniel C. Haynes

ABOUT THE AUTHOR

Daniel C. Haynes is a writer and educator whose work is guided by a profound connection to his Guyanese roots. Situated at the intersection of discipline and grace, his writing is imbued with richness and warmth.

Born in Guyana and refined in the concrete maze of New York City, Daniel blends the competitive spirit of an athlete with the lyrical soul of a poet. He has spent his life navigating the spaces between cultures, learning early that survival is a skill, but legacy is a choice.

A former athlete and coach, Daniel now brings that same philosophy of endurance and stewardship to the classroom and the page. As an educator, he mentors students to find their own voices; as a writer, he documents the journey of becoming.

He is the founder of *Turning Words Into Windows*® and the author of several collections of poetry, including *The Journey through the Wilderness* trilogy and the *Embers of Light & Shadows* trilogy. His work explores themes of identity, faith, resilience, and the quiet work of building a life that outlasts you.

Daniel resides in New York, where he continues to write, teach, and negotiate space on the couch with his two cats, Suki and Lucy.

Connect with Daniel at **www.twiw.us**